For the
RECORD

Bravery, Courage, Perseverance…
Extraordinary people, extraordinary acts.

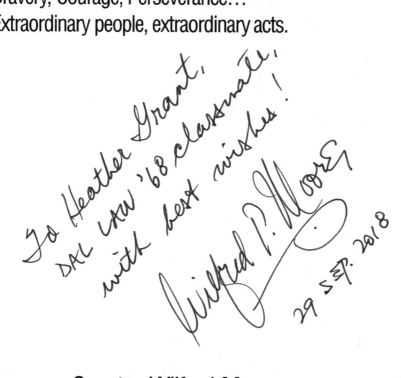

To Heather Grant,
DAL LAW '68 classmate!
with best wishes!
Wilfred P. Moore
29 SEP. 2018

Senator Wilfred Moore

MacIntyre Purcell Publishing Inc.

Copyright 2018 Senator Wilfred P. Moore

All rights reserved. No part of this book covered by the copyrights hereon may be reproduced or used in any form or by any means – graphic, electronic, or mechanical – without the prior written permission of the publisher. Any request for photocopying, recording, taping, or information storage and retrieval systems of any part of this book shall be directed in writing to the Canadian Reprography Collective, 379 Adelaide Street, West, Suite M1, Toronto, Ontario, M5V 1S5.

MacIntyre Purcell Publishing Inc.
194 Hospital Rd.
Lunenburg, Nova Scotia
B0J 2C0
(902) 640-3350

www.macintyrepurcell.com
info@macintyrepurcell.com

Printed and bound in Canada by Friesens 02

Design and layout: Alex Hickey
Cover design: Denis Cunningham
Front cover photo: Fred Chartrand
Back cover photo: Neil Valois

ISBN/CIP: 978-1-77276-104-7

Library and Archives Canada Cataloguing in Publication

Moore, Wilfred P.,
[Speeches. Selections]
      For the record / Wilfred P. Moore.

ISBN 978-1-77276-104-7 (softcover)

      1. Moore, Wilfred P. 2. Statesmen--Canada--Messages.
3. Legislators--Canada. 4. Canada. Parliament. Senate.
5. Speeches, addresses, etc., Canadian (English). I. Title.

FC636.M66A25 2018   328.71'02   C2017-907385-0

MacIntyre Purcell Publishing Inc. would like to acknowledge the financial support of the Government of Canada and the Nova Scotia Department of Tourism, Culture and Heritage.

This book is dedicated to
my parents, Betty and Wilfred, my heroes;
and my crew,
Jane Adams Ritcey, spouse and soulmate,
Nicholas Adams Thomas Moore, son,
and Alexandra Jane Ritcey Moore, daughter.

My deep gratitude for your patience during my many
absences while attending to my Senate
responsibilities, and for your steadfast love and
encouragement for me do the right thing
and to work for the greater good.

I hope this gives you some sense of what
I've been up to as I flew off to Ottawa.

Statement of Thanks

My time in the Senate of Canada ended at midnight on January 13, 2017, my 75th birthday being the following day and the mandatory retirement day for a senator. A senator has two months from her/his retirement date within which to pack up and move out of her/his office, and she/he is given one move to where her/his possessions are to be shipped.

It should be noted that I occupied Room 229 in the East Block, which abuts the original Cabinet Room. This office was formerly occupied by Sir John A. Macdonald, other prime ministers, and most notably Sir Charles Tupper and Joseph Howe — two outstanding Nova Scotians who gave us public education and freedom of the press, respectively. Needless to say, I did not need any encouragement to put in a solid work effort knowing that I was being overseen by those two "giant Nova Scotian ghosts."

Room 229 is at the northeast corner of the second floor hallway — it faces north and provides a full view of "The Famous Five" sculpture, by artist Barbara Paterson. That sculpture depicts the five women who won an appeal to the Privy Council in London, England, in 1929 in the famous "Persons Case" which ruled that women in Canada were no longer considered personal property, but, persons — and therefore eligible for consideration for appointment to the Senate of Canada.

To get back on track, as I began to review my files I came across the many Statements and Tributes which I had made over the past 20 years, many of which were brought to my attention by my then Administrative Assistant, Mrs. Marie J. Russell, a salt-of-the-earth Newfoundlander. We had been trying to keep track of those writings in a binder, which was begun by my immediate past Administrative Assistant, Ms. Lisa Fisher.

Hence, I express my sincere thanks to my Administrative Assistants, the late Doralen Amesbury, Lisa Fisher and Marie Russell. They all bore with me as I worked through drafts and re-writes so as to make my Statements and Tributes as inclusive and informative as possible, and to fit within the time limit of three minutes. A special "thank you" to Marie for helping to pull this all together.

I also wish to acknowledge my deep gratitude to my Legislative Assistant for nearly 15 years, Mr. Archibald J. Campbell, a proud Cape Bretoner from Irish Cove, Nova Scotia. Archie, who possesses finely-tuned political antennae, was a big help in researching the subject of these Statements and Tributes, confirming the accuracy of dates and facts.

Two other persons who were key to my efforts were D'Arcy McPherson and Janet Lovelady. These members of the Senate's Debates Directorate ensured that my Statements and Tributes were recorded accurately and sometimes uniquely, and provided me with the special covers for presentation and distribution.

I am also grateful for the work of Ms. Kim Laughren and Mr. Ayanleh Ismael, of Senate Publications, who pulled together the digital format in a timely way. And, my thanks to Mr. Charles Robert, Acting Clerk of the Senate, for his advice and guidance herein.

I wish to extend my sincere gratitude to those senators who, when asked, permitted me to take their place on the speaking list so that I could make my Statement or Tribute in a timely way. Their sensitivity to the importance of the timeliness of my Statement or Tribute was much appreciated.

The good folks at MacIntyre Purcell Publishing deserve my special appreciation, particularly John MacIntyre, publisher, who had the faith in this unique project, and Vernon Oickle, editor, who helped get this book into shape.

A final and most important "thank you" to the Right Honourable Jean Chrétien, the 20th Prime Minister of Canada, who appointed me to The Senate of Canada on September 26, 1996. I hope that I have honoured his judgement in making that appointment.

Statements and Tributes 1996-2016

Introduction

It's always nice after the end of the workday when the staff has gone home. When the telephone stops ringing. When one can have some quiet time to focus on a particular matter or file. Such was the situation on September 26, 1996. I was deep in thought in my office at the law firm of Chandler Moore in the Fairview section of Halifax, Nova Scotia, an area that I affectionately referred to as "beautiful Ward 9", which I had the honour to represent on Halifax City Council (1974-1980).

At about 5:45 p.m. I was startled out of my thought zone when the telephone rang. I answered the call to hear the voice of Mrs. Monique Bonder, Personal Assistant to our Prime Minister, the Right Honourable Jean Chrétien, P.C., Q.C., M.P., telling me that "the Boss" wished to speak to me. Let us all be clear — when the Prime Minister telephones, you take the call. Following our usual greetings our Prime Minister said he'd like me to come to the Senate, and asked what I thought of that idea. I replied that it would be an honour, whereupon he said ".... good, I'll announce the appointment tomorrow, keep it confidential till then. I've got to go to a meeting. Bye for now."

That telephone call changed my life. It vaulted me into a new career — a member of the Senate of Canada, one of our two legislative bodies; and, an opportunity to serve my province and our nation. It was all very intimidating. It meant a huge change in my work, in my place of work, in my time with my wife, Jane, and our children, Nicholas and Alexandra. I was the 801st Canadian to serve in the Senate. What a huge honour upon being sworn in on October 2, 1996. I thought about the Red Chamber and the long way it was from the jobs that I fortunately had as I worked my way through university.

It took me awhile to get onto the rhythm of the Senate, the sittings and agenda, the committee work, the caucus meetings, the parliamentary organizations, and, the opportunities. The opportunities to participate in the debate, whether in committee or in the Chamber as senators, working to forge legislation or reports for the greater good of Canada.

A very special opportunity is available to senators at the beginning of each sitting, immediately after Prayers. This opportunity appears on the Orders of Business (daily agenda) as "Senators' Statements", which, together with "Tributes", are provided for in the Rules of the Senate of Canada.

Early in my career as a Senator I saw the importance of that part of our daily agenda, and the opportunity it presented to give recognition to a citizen for her or his contribution to her or his respective community or to Canada, for a notable achievement or to bring attention to a career well spent.

So, then it was a matter of finding out how to get on that list of five senators. I learned it was a matter of contacting a legislative assistant in the office of the Deputy Leader of the Caucus in the Senate (in my case the Deputy Leader of the Liberal Party Caucus in the Senate, whether in government or in opposition) indicating one's wish to make a Statement and providing the topic.

Another factor is the convention. The list of senators wishing to make a statement is discussed and agreed to in the "Scroll Meeting" which is held between the deputy leaders of each party in the Senate every day in the morning on which the Senate meets. At the Scroll Meeting the agenda of matters and legislation to be considered in the Senate that day are discussed, thereby providing an indication or notice of those items that are of priority to each party. The five spots are shared between senators representing the government, the opposition and the independents. A copy of the list is provided to the Speaker of the Senate. Once the "Senator's Statements" item is reached on the agenda the Speaker of the Senate calls upon those senators in an alternating manner, beginning with a senator of the governing party.

At the beginning of each sitting of the Senate, the Usher of the Black Rod leads the parade of officials, led by the Speaker, into the Red Chamber. At the end of the parade is the Sergeant-at-Arms who bears the Mace and places it on The Table, which is located on the floor of the Senate in front of the Speaker's chair. Once the Mace is so placed and the Speaker sees a quorum (minimum of 15) of senators at their seats, the Speaker proceeds with the business of the Senate, beginning with Prayers. The Prayer is read in both official languages by the Speaker of the Senate.

It is very important that a senator limits the time for her or his Statement to three minutes as provided for in Rule 4-2 (3). One of the Reading Clerks seated at The Table keeps track of the time and stands about 10 seconds before the expiry of three minutes so that the speaking senator will know that she/he is nearing the end of her/his permitted time. Upon the expiry of the three minutes the Speaker calls upon the next senator on the list, and the sound system and microphone is then switched to the seat of that next senator.

Obviously, as a matter of public record, it is important to complete one's Statement within the permitted time and before the microphone service at her/his seat is cut and switched to another. There's a very practical reason as to why this is important — if the speaking senator intends to send a copy of her/his Statement to the person or entity mentioned therein, it is best if the official record includes that Statement in its entirety.

To ensure that my Statements were within the permitted three minutes I adopted a simple solution — I practiced and timed my Statements in my office before entering the Red Chamber and rising to make my Statement.

Once made, a Senator's Statement becomes part of the official record of Canada. It was my practice to send a letter noting this fact, together with a copy or copies of the subject Statement, to the persons or entity mentioned therein. Being part of the official record of Canada is unique and is treasured by those about whom I spoke, whether the persons and/or their families, and the entities and/or their officials, all of which was confirmed to me repeatedly in the many notes, telephone messages and e-mails which I received in response.

Over the years I tried to stay abreast of happenings in my community, in my province, in Canada and abroad. Through my practice of listening and reading I was often provided with information and materials, which made their way into my Statements and Tributes. As a senator from Nova Scotia my prime mission was to represent my province and minorities, and I attempted to do that in my Senate work. I also attempted to do that in my

Statements and Tributes; if the within appear so weighted, those are the reasons why. I have included Statements made by former Senate colleagues, Hon. Jane Cordy, Hon. Francis William ("Frank") Mahovlich and Hon. Nick Sibbeston, to give a little more spice to this book.

It is my hope that this text provides an insight into the inner workings of our Senate as relates to this specific section of its daily business. Most importantly, it gives me an opportunity to put on record the people and entities and their respective achievements and contributions to our communities, to Nova Scotia, to Canada and the world.

As we move past the 150th anniversary of the Confederation of Canada, I hope that this sharing of my Statements and Tributes will provide you with a sense of celebration, joy and fond memories. Vive le Canada!

International Special Olympics World Winter Games

Felicitations on Success of Games

Honourable senators, I should like to make a statement with respect to the World Special Olympics Winter Games which took place last week in the Toronto-Collingwood area. You may know that the Special Olympics drew 2,000 athletes and 3,000 volunteers from 72 countries throughout the world.

The Canadian team was made up of 82 athletes, young men and women. I am proud to say that two of those athletes were from Nova Scotia. One was a 22-year-old man from Shelburne, Martin Fudge, who worked and trained very hard. He practised last winter, when we did not have snow in Nova Scotia, by attaching foam rubber to the bottom of his snow shoes and working out on the country roads. He got his fighting weight down by 60 pounds and was successful in that he won three silver medals and one bronze.

Honourable senators, keep in mind that these athletes are mentally challenged, but they are very keen and disciplined, and they show great courage.

I now wish to tell you about Bonnie Conrad, 32, from Lunenburg. Bonnie is a speed skater. Until this past September, she was working out and using men's skates. Then she received a pair of speed skates, and has been practicing on them since then. She competed in three events in the Special Olympics. She won two silver medals. Her final event was a 333-meter event. She came from behind to win the gold. She won the gold for Canada, and she won the gold for herself. We are extremely proud of Bonnie and of her long-time coaches, Alice Bent from Bridgewater and Jane Ritcey from Lunenburg.

I am sure that all senators will join me in expressing our congratulations to the officials and the legion of volunteers who put on this world-class event and, more particularly, the athletes from Canada, who brought much goodwill and great honour to our beloved country.

— Tuesday, February 11, 1997

Congratulations to Lunenburg Yacht Club on Winning Chisholm Trophy

Honourable senators, I rise today to make a statement in recognition of the Lunenburg Yacht Club, which is located on Herman's Island on the shores of beautiful Prince Inlet within the waters of Mahone Bay, Nova Scotia. The spirit of the small community of Lunenburg and the high quality of the club's junior sailing program are well known. Its young sailors have gone on to become provincial, national and world champions in various classes of yachts.

Tomorrow, here in Ottawa, the Lunenburg Yacht Club will be honoured by the Canadian Yachting Association at its annual awards presentation. The club will receive the cherished Chisholm Trophy for staging the best Canadian regatta during the past sailing season. The regatta was the Canadian Youth/Highliner Sailing Championships held in mid-July.

The championships saw 225 young men and women from across Canada gather to compete in Lasers, Laser IIs, Bytes and Windsurfers. In addition to the keen competition, those youths also were treated to our legendary South Shore hospitality, and they made some lasting friendships.

Any event of this size requires leadership, dedication and volunteerism. I wish to extend sincere congratulations to Ron Whynacht, Commodore of the Lunenburg Yacht Club, his fellow officers and his crew of unselfish volunteers who staged this regatta.

I also wish to commend National Sea Products Limited of Lunenburg, the lead sponsor of this regatta, and the community spirit that it exhibited by contributing its resources to this Canadian championship event.

In closing, I would add that it is most fitting that the Lunenburg Yacht Club receive this award from the Canadian Yachting Association this year, which is the fiftieth anniversary of the founding of the club.

—*Thursday, October 23, 1997*

Zion Evangelical Lutheran Church, Lunenburg

Congratulations on 225th Anniversary

Honourable senators, I rise today to make a statement in recognition of the Zion Evangelical Lutheran Church in Lunenburg, Nova Scotia. This is the oldest Lutheran congregation in Canada, and this year they are celebrating their 225th anniversary.

Founded by original settlers from Germany, Zion Evangelical Lutheran Church has been, and continues to be, a cornerstone of family worship and social activity in the venerable Town of Lunenburg.

I wish to extend sincere congratulations to Reverend Douglas Moore, Pastor of Zion Evangelical Lutheran Church, and members of the congregation upon achieving this milestone of continuous fellowship and community good work, and I convey my sincere best wishes to Zion Evangelical Lutheran Church, its pastor and parishioners, for every success as we move into the next millennium.

—Tuesday, December 2, 1997

The Honourable M. Lorne Bonnell

Tribute on Retirement

Honourable senators, I rise today to make a statement in tribute to Senator M. Lorne Bonnell, who retired from this honourable chamber on January 4, 1998, upon the occasion of his 75th birthday.

Senator Bonnell entered public life in 1951 when, while still carrying on a busy medical practice, he was elected to the House of Assembly of Prince Edward Island. He was re-elected in general elections held in 1955, 1959, 1962, 1966 and 1970.

In addition to being an elected member, the good doctor also served his fellow Islanders as Minister of Health, Minister of Welfare, Minister of Tourism and Development, Minister Responsible for Housing, and Liberal house leader.

In 1965, he served as acting leader of the Liberal Party of Prince Edward Island. He knew how to get elected and stay elected.

On November 15, 1971, Dr. Bonnell was appointed to the Senate of Canada by the Right Honourable Pierre Elliott Trudeau. No doubt because of his medical training and experience, Senator Bonnell exhibited a strong interest in and deep concern for the youth of our country, their health and education.

Among the highlights of Senator Bonnell's distinguished career in the Senate must be his chairmanship of the Standing Senate Committee on Health, Welfare and Science, which produced a report in 1980 entitled "Child at Risk." That report and its contents are as much in vogue and as relevant today as they were 18 years ago.

Of equal importance was his chairmanship of the Special Committee on Post-Secondary Education which, in December 1997, produced a report that will be an important blueprint respecting the education of our youth and how we approach this very important issue in the years ahead.

Senator Bonnell's office in Room 265-E was a gathering spot for many senators from both sides of the house. There you would be treated to good conversation, lively stories and warm fellowship. The good doctor was quick to dispense medications or libations depending upon your need or request. After such sessions he revelled in frequenting the Cathay Restaurant for a meal of Chinese food chased with a beer.

On a personal note, when I came to this place in the fall of 1996, Senator Bonnell took me under his wing. He showed me around. He explained the operations and traditions of this honourable chamber, the functioning of its officers and the interests of the personalities seated herein. We two Maritimers quickly became good friends. I shall always be grateful for the interest that he took in me and the many courtesies he extended to me.

A devout family man of consummate energy, Senator Bonnell has returned to his beloved Murray River where he attends to his patients in his medical practice and oversees his various business interests.

With 20 years in the House of Assembly in Prince Edward Island, 27 years in the Senate of Canada, Senator Bonnell has provided a total of 47 years of service to his fellow Islanders and Canadians, a very distinguished record that required commitment, integrity and energy. Senator Bonnell has done his Island and Canada proud. We wish him well, we shall miss him.

—*Tuesday, February 17, 1998*

Bluenose

Seventy-Seventh Anniversary of Launch in Lunenburg, Nova Scotia

Honourable senators, I rise to make a statement with respect to a very important event that happened 77 years ago today. On March 26, 1921, the schooner *Bluenose* was launched at the yard of Smith & Rhuland in Lunenburg, Nova Scotia. The ship was designed by William J. Roué, a self-taught naval architect, of Halifax. She went on to become a highliner fisherman and sailed into our hearts and Canadian heritage forever as the undefeated "Queen of the North Atlantic," being victorious in every series of races in which she represented Canada against the United States of America for the coveted International Fishermen's Trophy.

Her legendary skipper was Captain Angus Walters of Lunenburg. I wish to pay tribute to Captain Walters and all of the men who sailed with him on *Bluenose*. Those men, the ship and her designer represented excellence in ship design, shipbuilding and seamanship, whether as fishermen or racers. Had these men not done what they did, there would be no *Bluenose* legend, and there certainly would not be a *Bluenose II*.

I, therefore, wish to make special mention of the surviving crew members of the original *Bluenose*: Don Bailly, Captain Perry Conrad, Robert Cook, Paul Crouse, Robert Crouse, Captain Ellswork Greek, Clement Hiltz, Captain Matthew Mitchell, Merrill Tanner and Paul Wentzell, all of Lunenburg; Harold Rafuse of Bridgewater; Clyde Eisnor of Mahone Bay, John Carter of Halifax, and Captain Claude Darrach of Herring Cove. These Nova Scotians were champions all.

It is also worthy of mention on this day that during the approaching summer, Canada Post Corporation will issue a stamp in recognition of William J. Roué and his design genius.

I can also advise that this summer the replica, *Bluenose II*, will depart her home port of Lunenburg, sail south, transit the Panama Canal, and make her way to British Columbia. She will sail in the waters of British Columbia for nearly one month in completion of her two-year national tour of Canada.

In closing, as you are aware, the Government of Canada announced last week various projects planned to celebrate the millennium. One of these projects is Tall Ships 2000, which will be the nautical event in Canada for that year and will see over 100 of the tall ships of the world gather in Halifax — always a hospitable liberty port. *Bluenose II* will participate in that event, which will draw tens of thousands of visitors to Nova Scotia. All senators will have received an invitation to Tall Ships 2000 in Halifax from July 19 to 24, 2000. I commend that historic event to you and suggest that you begin making your vacation plans now.

—Thursday, March 26, 1998

The Schooner *Bluenose II*

Honourable senators, I rise today to make a statement with respect to Nova Scotia's sailing ambassador of goodwill, the schooner *Bluenose II* — at 181 feet sparred length, the prettiest sailing ship in the world.

I have the pleasure of serving as the volunteer chairman of the *Bluenose II* Preservation Trust, the charity which has the mandate to maintain and operate this national icon.

Last year, the ship began a two-year tour of Canada which commenced on May 29, 1997, when she was the first ship to sail under the Confederation Bridge connecting New Brunswick and Prince Edward Island. *Bluenose II* sailed as far west as Thunder Bay and returned to her home port of Lunenburg on August 22, having travelled 5,000 nautical miles and visited 23 ports in Quebec, Ontario and the four Atlantic provinces. Over 162,000 proud Canadians visited her decks. The record for one day was set in Montreal when 11,200 people came aboard in nine and a half hours. Canadians love the ship, and we love to share her with them.

On July 24, 1997, *Bluenose II* visited Ville de La Baie upon the first anniversary of the great flood. Captain Wayne Walters, master of the vessel, delivered two mailbags full of postcards to the Museum de la Fiord. These postcards, many from Nova Scotian school children, contained messages of encouragement and inspiration to the people of that devastated area. The postcards now form part of the permanent exhibit of the museum.

This past Sunday evening, 1,000 people gathered on the wharf of Lunenburg to give a warm send-off to *Bluenose II* as she departed for British Columbia to complete the western portion of her tour. The ship will make stops in Bermuda and Jamaica, including one at sea near the reef of Île à Vache off the southwest tip of Haiti where the original *Bluenose* foundered on January 28, 1946.

From there, she will transit the Panama Canal, sail up the coast of Mexico and California and into British Columbia. The ship will sail in B.C. waters for one month, visiting eight ports. Her first port of call is Port Alberni on August 11. From there she will go north to Prince Rupert, west to Queen Charlotte City, down the inland passage to Gibsons, Nanaimo, Ganger, Victoria and Vancouver. She will leave Vancouver on September 11 for home, and is due back in Lunenburg on October 30. This voyage covers 15,000 nautical miles and is a historical trip for the ship and her fine co-ed crew.

I invite all honourable senators to follow the ship by visiting her web site at www.bluenose2.ns.ca.

—Wednesday, June 17, 1998

Halifax, Nova Scotia

Celebration of Birthday

Honourable senators, I rise today to make a statement with respect to the birthday of Halifax, Nova Scotia, my home town, which is to be celebrated on Sunday, June 21 next. That day marks the 249th anniversary of the day a new governor of Nova Scotia, Lieutenant Colonel Edward Cornwallis, 36, a slender, handsome, battle-hardened and incorruptible blue-blood from London, led a dozen ships carrying nearly 2,600 settlers up between the forests that flanked one of the world's finest natural harbours and founded what generations of Canadians would come to love as the city of Halifax.

The history of the city of Halifax is astonishingly rich. It is a history that not only Nova Scotians but all Canadians should celebrate. Halifax prepared the soil for the very sprouting of Canada. By the early 1800s, when "Muddy York," the future Toronto, had barely graduated from being a bunch of tents in a settlement of 70-odd cabins, Halifax was not only the bastion of British power in North America and the strongest fortress outside Europe, but a bustling, cosmopolitan port of 10,000 residents boasting architectural treasures like Government House, the town clock, St. Paul's Church, as well as three newspapers, crowded theatres, a taste for balls, banquets, fireworks and parades, and a reputation as the home of beautiful, bejeweled and fashionably dressed women.

I am not knocking Toronto, but for swashbuckling, rip-snorting, seafaring, warfaring, international history — for heroes, scoundrels, adventurers and buccaneers — Toronto cannot come within a nautical mile of little old Halifax.

No city in Canada felt the deprivation, agony, horror, excitement and thunder of the Second World War more than Halifax. No city was more in the war or aroused so much affection and loathing amongst soldiers and sailors from across the nation — and I have not even mentioned the *Titanic*, the Halifax explosion or the VE Day riots.

To His Worship Mayor Walter R. Fitzgerald, the councillors and citizens of the city affectionately known as "The Warden of the North," I say happy birthday. In doing so, may I add words of appreciation and encouragement to Mr. Jack Keith and his committee of volunteers who are busy at work preparing for Halifax's 250th birthday next year.

I acknowledge the help of the noted writer Mr. Harry Bruce in these remarks.

—Thursday, June 18, 1998

The Late Harold Edwin Joseph Pelham

Tribute

Honourable senators, I rise today to pay tribute to Harold Edwin Joseph Pelham, a fellow Haligonian who departed this life at home, in peace, and surrounded by his loving family on Tuesday, October 13, 1998, two days after his 73rd birthday.

Born in the north end of Halifax, Harold served in the Royal Canadian Navy and in World War II; he fought in the Battle of the Atlantic, for which he was awarded the Atlantic Star and other decorations. After the war Harold worked as an electrical estimator at the HMCS dockyard in Halifax until 1967, when he founded his own business, Pelham Electric and Refrigeration Limited. He was a devout family man, a man of deep faith and a fervent small businessman.

Harold was also a man of untold generosity. For nearly 40 years he coached and sponsored minor hockey teams, and minor and senior baseball teams in Halifax, many of which were Nova Scotia champions. In 1976 the National Baseball Team of Cuba visited Halifax. When others shied away, Harold stepped forward and sponsored that visit. He did so not for personal recognition but for the pure sport of it. He wanted to see how the young men who made up his Pelham Electric senior team would fare against the Cubans. The visitors won; however, Harold's team was never out of the game. Later that day, he and his wife, Mary, hosted a reception for the Cuban team and coaches at their Purcell's Cove home. Despite health problems that would have slowed most, Harold never wavered in his commitment to, and support of, the youth of metropolitan Halifax.

The mass in celebration of Harold's life was held in St. Theresa's Roman Catholic Church in Halifax's north end, one block from where Harold grew up. St. Theresa's swelled with family, friends and athletes — athletes both young and old, from all walks of life, all of us having benefited from Harold's lessons in teamwork, generosity, perseverance and pursuit of excellence.

In his homily, Father Terrance O'Toole, a boyhood friend and adult confidant, echoed Harold's obituary, which read in part:

> He shared his opinions and modest wealth
> generously. No one who asked was denied.

When the Lord created Harold Pelham, he hit a grand slam home run. It is people like Harold Pelham who make Canada the wonderful motherland that she is.

Thus it is with the utmost respect for the passing of a good man that we convey our deepest sympathy to Harold's wife, Mary, and their children, Patricia, Marie, Theresa, Harold Jr., James and Donald. We thank them for sharing Harold with us.

—Wednesday, October 21, 1998

Chester Brass Band

Celebration of One Hundred and
Twenty-fifth Anniversary

Honourable senators, I rise today to make a statement in recognition of the Chester Brass Band, of the Village of Chester, Nova Scotia, which celebrated its 125 years of music-making with an afternoon anniversary concert at the Chester Area Middle School on Sunday, November 8, 1998.

Since the band was first organized in 1873, all of its members have been volunteers. For more than 100 years, the members of the band were from Chester proper. From 1981, the band grew from a hometown band to a band of 30 players which now includes talented musicians from other South Shore communities, the Annapolis Valley and Halifax.

The band has always enjoyed the support of the nearly 1,000 residents of Chester, whose donations have assisted in the acquisition of instruments, sheet music and uniforms. The band regularly performs concerts at the Chester bandstand during the summer months.

It should be noted that the band performs in many communities in Nova Scotia, often assisting in the raising of funds for local charities and community organizations. In addition, the band has performed at other events worthy of mention including the G-7 Economic World Leaders Conference in Halifax, the World Conference of Girl Guides at Wolfville, concerts commemorating the *Bluenose* and The Fisheries Museum of the Atlantic at Lunenburg, and the Lieutenant-Governor's garden party at Halifax. They have also played with the Nova Scotia Symphony in Halifax.

The Chester Brass Band has competed five times in the North American Brass Band Championships held in Washington, Toronto and West Chester, Pennsylvania. It has earned a third place and four second-place marks. The band is currently conducted by Ken Foote of Bridgewater, who, in the 1995 championship, received the top mark for euphonium soloists.

In closing, I wish to commend the Chester Brass Band, its members and conductors, past and present alike, for the joyful music they have provided to the village and beyond for 125 years, and for the well-deserved recognitions they have earned for themselves. I extend every good wish to the band in its future activities.

—Wednesday, November 18, 1998

F. W. Schumacher

Father Christmas of Northern Ontario Town

Hon. Francis William Mahovlich: Honourable senators, this being the festive season, I thought it would be appropriate to tell you a Christmas story that I experienced in my childhood, and how fortunate I was to be born in Canada, and in Northern Ontario in particular.

In 1945, my father thought it was time to get off the farm so we moved to a little town called Schumacher. The "Mr. Schumacher" that the town was named after was our very own Santa Claus.

He came from Holland and the family settled in Waco, Texas. Eventually, they moved up to Columbus, Ohio. Mr. Schumacher then went to the University of Columbus. It was during Prohibition that he entered the business world. His business was selling cough syrup. However, that cough syrup happened to be 45 per cent alcohol. He amassed a fortune. He sold it not only by the truckload but also by the trainload.

Well, Prohibition ended. Mr. Schumacher's business closed and he had to look for another business. He picked up a newspaper and saw that there was a gold strike in Northern Ontario, so off he went. He bought a mine, and subdivided the area into a town called Schumacher, which was named after himself, F.W. Schumacher, as was the public and high school that was located in the town.

During his time there, he did very well. He was very fortunate. He went to Europe and began to purchase great art. If you visit the art museum located in Columbus, Ohio, you will be able to see his art collection.

All the students and all the children in the area, which had a population of about 3,500, would receive a gift at Christmas from Mr. Schumacher — whether it be a sleigh, a pair of skates, a hockey stick or a hockey sweater. One year, I received a hockey sweater — a Detroit Red Wings hockey sweater — and a pair of socks. I immediately changed my allegiance from the Toronto Maple Leafs over to the Detroit Red Wings because of that sweater!

My point is that this man was extremely generous. He passed away in 1957. About three or four years ago, I had a chance to visit with some of the friends with whom I went to school. Some of them are now principals and teachers there. They told me another story involving the Schumacher family's generosity. The town ran out of funds for the Christmas gift-giving tradition because of inflation, so they approached the Schumacher family, who now live in Los Angeles. They were presented with another $3 million so that the Christmas tradition that was initiated by Mr. Schumacher could continue. Even today, a young boy in the little town of Schumacher receives a gift from the late F.W. Schumacher. Indeed, the spirit of Christmas is alive and well in the Town of Schumacher!

—*Wednesday, December 9, 1998*

Curling

Triumph of Nova Scotia Rink at
National Mixed Championship

Honourable senators, I rise today to make a statement in recognition of the achievement of Paul Flemming and his rink, of the Mayflower Curling Club in Halifax, Nova Scotia, upon winning the Canadian Mixed Curling Championship at Victoria, British Columbia, on Sunday, January 17, 1999. The winning rink included Paul as skip, Colleen Jones as mate, lead Monica Moriarty, and second Tom Fetterly. In Cinderella fashion, the Nova Scotia rink downed Ontario in a sudden death semi-final on Sunday afternoon and went on to win the national title over Prince Edward Island that evening.

In addition to this championship, Paul Flemming was named the all-star skip in this national event, and he was also awarded the Sportsmanship Award, a recognition voted upon by all players. It is also worthy of note that this title marked the fourth such in the past seven years to be won by Nova Scotia.

I extend our sincere congratulations to Paul Flemming and the members of his championship squad.

—Wednesday, February 3, 1999

National Women's Curling Championship

Congratulations to Colleen Jones Rink, Halifax on Winning

Honourable senators, I rise today to make a statement in recognition of the Colleen Jones rink from the Mayflower Curling Club of Halifax, Nova Scotia, who won the National Women's Curling Championship this past weekend in Charlottetown, Prince Edward Island. Our congratulations go to the skip, Colleen, and the other members of that winning foursome, mate Kim Kelly, second Mary-Anne Waye and lead Nancy Delahunt, who persevered during the entire week, through the pressure of a near-perfect tournament record, to win a title which had not been captured by a Maritime team for 17 years — and yes, it was a Colleen Jones-led rink who won that championship back in 1982. It should also be noted that Kim Kelly was named the most valuable player for the tournament.

It is with much pride that we wish Colleen Jones and her team good luck as Canada's representatives in the World Curling Championship to be hosted by Saint John, New Brunswick, April 3 to 9 next.

There were other winners this past weekend: the hosts of this remarkably successful championship — the people of Prince Edward Island. Our congratulations also go to the more than 1,000 volunteers who pulled together in Charlottetown to make this Scott Tournament of Hearts — one of Canada's most prestigious sporting events — such a huge success. My colleague Senator Callbeck joins me in extending these most sincere congratulations to those Islanders.

Time and again, the people of Prince Edward Island have shown an amazing ability to rise above whatever shortcomings may be associated with this small population to stage the best possible events, be they regional, national or international. The more than 50,000 fans who attended this week-long championship and the millions who viewed it on television are testament to the high quality of the efforts of those volunteers. They have our heartfelt respect and gratitude.

—*Wednesday, March 3, 1999*

Canadian Intercollegiate Athletic Union Basketball Championships 1999

Congratulations to Saint Mary's University Huskies on Winning

Honourable senators, I rise today to make a statement in recognition of the achievement of the men's varsity basketball team of Saint Mary's University of Halifax, Nova Scotia.

This past Sunday afternoon, the basketball Huskies, ranked number seven in the nation, won the Canadian Intercollegiate Athletic Union championship in a thrilling 73-69 overtime victory over the number one ranked Alberta Golden Bears in a tournament played before a crowded Metro Centre in Halifax. This marked the first time such title has been decided in overtime.

Saint Mary's last won this national title 20 years ago. Ross Quackenbush, coach of the Huskies, was a member of those 1978 and 1979 teams. It should be noted that Cory Janes of Middleton, Nova Scotia, who plays centre with the Huskies, was named most valuable player of this year's tournament. As an alumnus and one serving on the board of governors of Saint Mary's University, it is with grace and pride that we savour this gutsy victory, a victory that also speaks well of the strength and spirit of our Atlantic Universities Athletic Association.

This win is also a confirmation of the balancing of academic and athletic excellence at Saint Mary's, founded in 1802 and a university where tradition meets the future. We heartily congratulate Coach Quackenbush, his team and their legion of supporters.

We also extend our thanks and gratitude to Peter Halpin, a former varsity basketball player at Saint Mary's and a member of the Huskies 1973 national championship team, and his crew of unselfish volunteers for their commitment and hard work in organizing and convening this first-class national athletic event.

—*Tuesday, March 23, 1999*

The Late Francis V. Baldwin

Tribute

Honourable senators, I rise to pay tribute to Francis V., or "Frank" Baldwin, a fellow Haligonian who departed this life on Friday, April 30, 1999, at 78 years of age.

Frank was known for his infectious enthusiasm, his great love of his church, St. Mary's Basilica, and the music which graced it, which was enhanced by Frank's fine tenor voice and his more than 40 years of membership in its choir. Mostly, however, he was known for his passion for the game of basketball. Indeed, Frank Baldwin was "Mr. Basketball" in Nova Scotia.

A member of the Nova Scotia Sports Heritage Hall of Fame and the Canadian Basketball Hall of Fame, Frank's coaching career began in a Halifax church league in 1939. In 1949-50, he coached Queen Elizabeth High School of Halifax to the national juvenile championship. In 1952, he moved to Saint Mary's University where he built the program from the ground up.

This past March, I spoke in this chamber in recognition of the Canadian Intercollegiate Athletic Union National Basketball Championship, won by Saint Mary's Huskies. That victory was one of the fine crop of successes which resulted from the seeds planted by Frank Baldwin in the early 1950s, and nurtured by him in the years following.

In 1963, he left Saint Mary's to work as director of the Canadian Martyrs Parish Centre. In 1971, he became the first provincial coach of the Nova Scotia Amateur Basketball Association. He was named the sport's provincial development coordinator soon thereafter, a position which he joyfully filled until his retirement in 1986.

Frank coached Nova Scotia's 1971 and 1975 men's Canada Games basketball teams, and was an assistant coach with our national team in 1975 and at the 1976 Olympics. He received the Merit Award from the National Association of Basketball Coaches for outstanding service to basketball in Canada.

Permit me to share with honourable senators the remarks made by others upon Frank's passing. Bob Hayes, the legendary athletic director of Saint Mary's University said:

> Besides coaching at Saint Mary's, Frank coached
> two basketball teams at high school and managed
> the bookstore and canteen. I told him last
> week that Saint Mary's now has 300 people to
> replace you.

Bruce Reynolds, president of Basketball Nova Scotia, said:

> There is no person who has done as much for
> basketball in the province of Nova Scotia. No one
> knew more about the game than Frank, and he
> had a completely unselfish way of sharing his
> knowledge, which he did out of love of the game
> and love for people in the game. He was like a
> Pied Piper of basketball. The sport has lost a
> builder without parallel and a friend without
> parallel. It's a sad day for basketball.

Brian Heaney, who coached at Saint Mary's after Frank, and had Frank with him as an assistant coach at the 1976 Olympics, recalling the man he describes as a true ambassador of the game, said:

> He travelled worldwide and brought goodwill and
> concern for his fellow man. I'm sure he never left
> an enemy in the world. He was revered within the
> coaching community in Canada. To a man at the
> CIAU level, he had an enormous level of support
> and friendship. He will be sorely missed and
> wonderfully remembered.

Joel Jacobson, who worked with Frank at Sport Nova Scotia, and who is a Halifax newspaper columnist, said:

> He put his heart and soul into basketball, and was
> very conscientious and worked long hours for the
> betterment of the game. A legend is gone.

Finally, Steve Konchalski, head basketball coach at St. Francis Xavier University and a former national men's team coach, who played against Frank's team at Saint Mary's in 1962, said:

> He was a giant of a man. He never coached me,
> but he was still my coach - he had such a positive
> influence on my life. Frank was all about helping
> young people - he touched the lives of so many
> young people in so many ways - it's a legacy to
> us all.

It is with the utmost respect that we convey our deepest sympathies to Frank Baldwin's immediate family and to the legion of basketball players who benefited from his unselfish sharing of his knowledge and love of that game.

—Thursday, May 6, 1999

Nova Scotia

International and National Awards
Won by Citizens of Lunenburg

Honourable senators, I rise today to make a statement in recognition of the international and national awards recently earned by the Town of Lunenburg, Nova Scotia and her citizens.

On Friday, November 5, 1999, Lunenburg was presented with the Port of the Year Award by the American Sail Training Association of Newport, Rhode Island, at its twenty-seventh annual meeting held in Boston. Members of ASTA are from across the Americas. This award is presented annually to the community that demonstrates significant support of ASTA and recognizes and encourages sail training. It is the first time that the award has been presented to a Canadian port.

At that same meeting, Captain Daniel P. Moreland, Master of the barque *Picton Castle*, of Lunenburg, was honoured as ASTA's sail trainer of the year. Captain Moreland successfully circumnavigated the world in *Picton Castle* with a crew who were mostly novices when they departed Lunenburg in November 1977 for their 18-month historic odyssey.

Yesterday, Marq de Villiers of Lunenburg won the 1999 Governor General's Literary Award for non-fiction with his book entitled *Water*, a superb text about this precious resource of our earth. Mr. de Villiers generously donated one-half of his $10,000 prize to Lunenburg's library to assist it in its good work.

We congratulate and salute the Town of Lunenburg, Mayor Laurence Mawhinney and councillors, her shipwrights, marine blacksmiths, sailmakers and hospitable townsfolk. We congratulate and applaud Captain Daniel P. Moreland and Marq de Villiers for their undertakings and the awards they achieved.

—Wednesday, November 17, 1999

Nova Scotia

Lunenburg Asthma Care Centre

In recognition of the Lunenburg Asthma Care Centre, which is located in the Fishermen's Memorial Hospital in Lunenburg, Nova Scotia. Commenced just four years ago, the centre was recently named the top Canadian clinic of its kind in a study done by Queen's University of Kingston, Ontario, as the best of eight asthma clinics in Canada at treating adolescent patients.

Not only has the centre dramatically improved the lifestyles of its child and adult patients, it has saved the health care system approximately $650,000 per year. Since opening in 1996, the centre has worked with about 700 clients, more than 400 of them children. The centre has been responsible for reducing the number of emergency room visits, decreasing hospital admissions and shortening patient stays in hospital. Fewer children are missing school and fewer parents are missing work because their children are sick.

Nova Scotia has the second highest incidence of asthma in Canada. Prince Edward Island has the highest. Doctors are still trying to determine why.

What distinguishes this centre from others in Halifax, Kentville and Yarmouth is that it is dedicated exclusively to asthma. The prime function of the centre is to teach people how to control their asthma instead of asthma controlling them.

The centre's success is due to its one-on-one patient care, stressing education through self-assessment and self-help. Other centres have self-help groups or videos rather than the one-on-one teaching offered here.

We commend the centre's medical director, Dr. Tony Atkinson, and his dedicated staff. We wish them and their patients continued success as they pursue and expand their national standard-setting asthma treatment program.

—*Wednesday, February 16, 2000*

Scott Tournament of Hearts

Nova Scotia—Congratulations to Winning Rink

Honourable senators, last Wednesday, my colleague Senator Callbeck spoke in this place about the Shelly Bradley rink from Prince Edward Island, which was then leading the Scott Tournament of Hearts Canadian Women's Curling Championship in Sudbury, Ontario. I am tickled to report that despite P.E.I.'s strong start, this championship was won by the Colleen Jones rink of the Mayflower Curling Club in Halifax, Nova Scotia, in a gritty eleventh-end comeback victory over Team Canada, the Kelley Law rink of British Columbia. With this third championship, Colleen Jones joins the elite of Canada's woman curlers, Manitoba's Connie Laliberte, Saskatchewan's Vera Pezer and the late Sandra Schmirler, all three-time winners of the event.

We congratulate skip Colleen and her teammates, lead Nancy Delahunt, second Mary-Anne Waye, third Kim Kelly, spare Lanie Peters and coach Ken Bagnell. We wish them well as they represent Canada at the women's World Curling Championships scheduled for Lausanne, Switzerland, this coming March 31 to April 8th.

—Thursday, March 1, 2001

World Women's Curling Championship

Nova Scotia—Congratulations to Winning Rink

Honourable senators, last month, I spoke in recognition of the Canadian Women's Curling Championship victory of Colleen Jones and her rink from the Mayflower Curling Club in Halifax, Nova Scotia. I am delighted to report that these Canadian champions also won the World Women's Curling Championship in a 5-2 victory over Sweden at Lausanne, Switzerland, on April 7, 2001.

In speaking to this superb effort, I find it noteworthy that *The Globe and Mail*, which proclaims itself to be Canada's national newspaper, gave markedly more coverage to the losing men's rink than it did to our victorious women's rink. Such unbalanced reporting, regardless of the medium, does a disservice to our female athletes. Only with equal coverage can we recognize with honour the efforts of our female champions. Only with equal coverage can we encourage our young female athletes to work to attain championship levels of performance. A female Canadian champion is a Canadian champion. A female world champion from Canada is a world champion.

I am sure that all honourable senators join me in congratulating Skip Colleen Jones and her teammates: lead Nancy Delahunt, second Mary-Anne Waye, third Kim Kelly, alternate Laine Peters and coach Ken Bagnell. We extend to them our thanks for the honour they brought to Canada.

—*Tuesday, April 24, 2001*

Mr. Jean Béliveau
The Honourable E. Leo Kobler

Congratulations on Receiving Doctoral Degrees from Saint Mary's University

Honourable senators, I wish to advise that on October 4, 2001, Jean Béliveau was awarded an Honorary Degree of Doctor of Civil Law by Saint Mary's University of Halifax, Nova Scotia at its fall convocation in recognition of his stellar contribution to our national game during his all-star career as a member of the Montreal Canadiens and for his unselfish community work.

In his citation, Archbishop Austin Burke said:

> Mr. Béliveau's life has been a model for others on the ice and off the ice.

Dr. Béliveau joins another esteemed recent graduate of my *alma mater*, our colleague Senator E. Leo Kolber, who was awarded an Honorary Degree of Doctor of Laws by Saint Mary's at its convocation held on May 15, 2001, in recognition of his leadership in business and politics, including spearheading the recent changes to our capital gains tax regime, and for his tireless and generous community work, particularly on behalf of the Jewish General Hospital in Montreal.

We commend Saint Mary's University for bestowing these most deserved recognitions, and we congratulate Drs. Béliveau and Kolber, two of the finest captains to ever compete respectively in the rinks and boardrooms of Canada.

—*Thursday, October 18, 2001*

The Honourable Leonce Mercier

Tributes on Retirement

Honourable senators, I rise to join in the tributes in recognition of the Honourable Léonce Mercier. I have known him for nearly 20 years. Over that time, I have observed him in action as a most astute political organizer, and I have had the pleasure of working with him on numerous campaigns. He was always courteous, always energetic, always loyal and always fun.

He brought those strengths to the Senate during his service to Canada in this place, and those strengths and his generous nature equipped him well to serve as a most congenial Government Whip.

We shared many laughs and successes over the years, and I shall miss him. I thank him for his friendship.

"Bonne chance, mon ami," to you and your family in the years ahead.

—Wednesday, October 24, 2001

Nova Scotia

Lunenburg—Burning of St. John's Anglican Church

Honourable senators, late in the night of October 31 or early in the morning of November 1, some person or persons tore a hole in the heart of Lunenburg, Nova Scotia. They did so by deliberately setting afire St. John's Anglican Church, a fire that raged for one-half day and consumed a structure of absolute beauty and peacefulness, a structure of refuge, a structure of tranquility and of steadfast worship. An elderly parishioner told me yesterday that he has not seen the mood of the town so darkened since the days of World War II.

St. John's was built in 1753 by German Protestants who were sent to Lunenburg to settle the seaport. Those builders were shipwrights, millers, fishermen and farmers. Their work resulted in a wonderful church with wooden knees, arches and rounded ceilings, which moved visitors to remark that it was like being inside a ship.

Honourable senators, for nearly 250 years, St. John's was the object of devout care and stewardship. It was a place of assembly, celebration and remembrance for our forefathers and today's parish families, including my own. Little remains of this National Historic Site — the second oldest Anglican church in Canada.

Honourable senators, I did say "little." I did not say "nothing." Remarkably, the font, the altar, the processional cross and some other precious pieces survived.

We are hopeful that the authorities will apprehend those who committed this senseless act of destruction and that the full weight of the law will be brought to bear upon them. We are prayerful that St. John's will rise again. We are confident that her parishioners harbour the will and can harvest the resources from across Canada to build a replica around those surviving pieces of worship.

—Tuesday, November 6, 2001

Vanier Cup

Congratulations to St. Mary's Huskies on Win

Honourable senators, I rise to extend congratulations to the varsity football team, the Huskies, of St. Mary's University in Halifax, Nova Scotia, upon their 42-to-16 victory over the University of Manitoba Bisons to win the Vanier Cup, emblematic of Canadian university football supremacy, at the SkyDome in Toronto this past Saturday evening. With this win, the Huskies completed a perfect 11-to-0 season, during which they outscored the opposition 608 to 66 and did not allow a single rushing touchdown, clearly a historic performance in the annals of Canadian university football.

We commend and respect coach Brian Dobie and the Bisons for the high calibre performance that they brought to this championship game.

We Santamarians are proud of the Huskies, their coach, Blake Nill, and his assistants, our athletic director, Larry Uteck, our athletic director emeritus, Bob Hayes, who started this exceptional football program on a bootstring budget in 1958, and to the silent hand of Father John J. Hennessey, S.J. We congratulate Ryan Jones, the team's composed quarterback, for his stellar performance, which earned him the game's Most Valuable Player on Offence award, and defensive lineman Kyl Morrison, who won the Bruce Coulter Trophy as most outstanding defensive player.

Well done, Huskies! You are our heroes.

—Tuesday, December 4, 2001

Scott Tournament Of Hearts Champions

Congratulations to Colleen Jones Rink

Honourable senators, on March 1, 2001, I rose in this place to extend congratulations to Colleen Jones and her rink from the Mayflower Curling Club in Halifax, Nova Scotia, upon winning the Scott Tournament of Hearts: Canadian Women's Curling Championship, being the third win by skip Colleen in that event.

This past weekend in Brandon, Manitoba, Colleen Jones and her rink defeated Saskatchewan's Sherry Anderson 8-5, to win this national title. In so doing, Colleen Jones made Canadian curling history by winning an unprecedented fourth national championship as skip.

We congratulate skip Colleen, lead Nancy Delahunt, second Mary-Anne Waye, third Kim Kelly, alternate Laine Peters and coach Ken Bagnell. One cannot say enough about this superb team of female athletes who have won three national titles together while managing to juggle their family lives, careers and personal pursuits. They are our heroines.

I know that all honourable senators join me in wishing this rink every success as they represent Canada in defence of their World Women's Curling Championship title, scheduled for Bismarck, North Dakota, starting on April 6.

It was good to see the front page and headline, reporting that this female athletic triumph deservedly received in the local and national press.

—Thursday, March 7, 2002

Nova Scotia

Greenwood—Close Out of 434 Bluenose Squadron

Honourable senators, yesterday I attended the ceremony commemorating the close out of 434 Bluenose Squadron, Combat Support, at 14 Wing, Greenwood, Nova Scotia. The ceremony was overseen by Her Honour Myra A. Freeman, Lieutenant-Governor of Nova Scotia, His Royal Highness The Prince Michael of Kent, Vice Chief of Defence, Staff Lieutenant-General G.E.C. Macdonald and Chief of the Air Staff, Lieutenant-General L.C. Campbell. This historic squadron was formed at Tholthorpe, England, on 13 June, 1943, as a bomber unit flying Halifax Vs and then Lancasters. During World War II, the squadron flew some 2,600 combat sorties, dropped 10,575 tonnes of bombs and mines and 68 crewmembers made the ultimate sacrifice.

The squadron's original complement of personnel contained a large number of Maritimers, and thus it was an obvious choice when the squadron adopted the schooner *Bluenose* as both its crest and nickname. Besides acquiring 150 individual declarations, the Bluenosers received 11 battle honours.

In addition to the Halifax and Lancaster aircraft, 434 has flown the F-86 Sabre, CF-104 Starfighter, CF-5 Freedom Fighter, C-144 Challenger and the T-33 Silver Star, the mighty Thunderbird. The tail fins of these aircraft have all borne the image of *Bluenose*.

The exemplary service of 434 Bluenose Squadron has made a significant contribution to the pursuit and protection of the precious freedoms we enjoy as a democratic people. Canada shall always be in their debt. We shall never forget. In the words of Colonel G.M.A. Morey, 14 Wing Commander:

> Like *Bluenose*, these schooners of the sky represent excellence, and they are true champions.

The motto of this squadron is "We Conquer in the Heights." They have certainly done that. Moreover, they have conquered our hearts.

The squadron has been disbanded three times in the past. It will be disbanded again on 15 July, 2002. However, we should keep a lookout because, I am sure, this historic unit will again be reactivated in the future.

To Lieutenant-Colonel J.R. Turner, Commanding Officer of 434 Bluenose Squadron, Combat Support, and the men and women of his crew, we say "Three Cheers!" for a job well done, and we wish the skipper and his Bluenosers the very best of health and happiness in the future.

—Monday, March 25, 2002

The *Bluenose*

Honourable senators, on this day in 1921, a significant part of Canada's maritime culture and the seafaring heritage of Nova Scotia began with the launch of the schooner *Bluenose* from the Smith & Rhuland Shipyard at Lunenburg. During the next 19 days her two masts were stepped, she was rigged by Tom Mader of Mahone Bay, she was outfitted for fishing and, on April 15, 1921, she set sail for the Grand Banks. *Bluenose* was a highliner fisherman and a champion racer, and she has come to represent excellence in ship design, shipbuilding and seamanship.

Since 1994, I have served as the volunteer Chairman of the *Bluenose II* Preservation Trust, a not-for-profit society and charity of Lunenburg, with the mandate to maintain and operate *Bluenose II*, a replica of the original *Bluenose*. In May 1996, our Trust began its correspondence with the Royal Canadian Mint in an effort to convince the mint that the fully-rigged fishing schooner on the reverse side of the 10-cent coin of Canada is *Bluenose*. On Friday, March 15, 2002, the mint announced that it has officially recognized *Bluenose* as the design on our 10-cent coin.

I am delighted that the work of our Trust has resulted in this official recognition of *Bluenose* by the mint. I am especially happy for the family of the late William J. Roué, her designer; for the shipwrights of Lunenburg who built her; for the men of Lunenburg who fished and sailed in her, particularly the family of the late Captain Angus J. Walters, her legendary skipper; for her crew, some of whom still reside in Lunenburg; and for the people of Canada, for whom she proudly sailed victoriously.

The lure and charm of this ship continues. Just last month, Trent Evans, icemaker of Edmonton, placed a dime bearing *Bluenose* to mark the centre ice dot in the hockey rink at Salt Lake City, one half inch below the loonie that he also placed there. Our women's and men's hockey teams won gold medals at those Olympics, buoyed up by the luck of *Bluenose*.

—*Tuesday, March 26, 2002*

The Late Doctor John Savage, O.C.

Tributes

Honourable senators, I rise today to pay tribute to John Savage, a medical doctor who served as Liberal Premier of Nova Scotia from 1993 to 1997 and who passed away yesterday.

A native of Wales, John Savage chose Nova Scotia for himself and his family in 1966. His community work as a physician in Dartmouth, particularly in the largely black community of North Preston, is legendary. When he left the premier's office, he resumed with great energy that humanitarian work, which saw him devote his knowledge and expertise to those less fortunate in Russia and Africa.

When John Savage took over the administration of Nova Scotia, our province was a financial basket case, with a deficit of $617 million. His mission was to put our financial house in order. Through financial reforms, the good doctor's sometimes tough medicine resulted in a reduction in the provincial debt for the first time since 1965.

Among his many accomplishments, one of the most outstanding, in my opinion, was his creation of a province-wide emergency ambulance system, one that has become a model across North America, indeed, around the world.

A man of integrity and vision, John Savage's tough love was both timely and necessary for Nova Scotia. In an interview last month, he said the following: "A more astute politician would have staged major changes over two terms, not in one... that would have been the wiser course." As true as those words are in the political world, that luxury was not available to John Savage, given the real-world financial situation he was facing as our premier.

We shall always respect and honour his unselfish integrity. It has been a rough year for the Savage family. John Savage's wife, Margaret, passed away only six weeks ago, also of cancer. Our deepest and heartfelt sympathy go to their seven children, and we thank them for sharing their wonderful parents with us.

-Wednesday, May 14, 2003

The Late John R. (Johnny) Cash

Honourable senators, I rise today to pay tribute to John R. Cash, late, of Hendersonville, Tennessee, publicly known as Johnny Cash or the "Man in Black." Born in Kingsland, Arkansas, on February 26, 1932, he departed this life on September 12, 2003, at 71 years of age at Nashville, Tennessee.

Johnny Cash began his career in the music business in 1956 at Sun Records in Nashville. From that beginning, he was always at the forefront of country music, whether as a songwriter, musician, recording artist or television show host. A generous man, he gave opportunity to numerous new performers and provided work for many other performers, known and unknown alike. Along the way, like each one of us, he fought his demons. He strove to be true to his cotton farm roots and his strong family values.

I met Johnny Cash in 1958 in Halifax during his first Canadian tour. I always attended his shows, sometimes went to rehearsals, and always went backstage before showtime to welcome him back to Nova Scotia and to wish him well. He never forgot his fans.

His last visit to Halifax was in 1993 with the "Highwaymen" tour. We got together backstage before that show at the Halifax Metro Centre, a performance that I enjoyed from great seats — appropriately, in the penalty box, which I shared with a lifelong fan of Johnny's, my friend Tom Faulkner.

Johnny had a strong affection for Canada, and not just for touring and vacationing. In 1968, during a performance in London, Ontario, he proposed on stage to June Carter, a member of the Carter family, the legendary first family of country music. They married later that year, and for her he walked the line.

Over his 47-year career, Johnny Cash was the ultimate story-teller. He entertained people with tales of their greed and their goodness, their losses and their loves, their tragedies and their triumphs. In an Associated Press interview in 1987, June gave perhaps the finest recognition to her husband when she said:

> There's a lot of power to him. I've seen him on
> shows with people with a No. 1 record or a lot of

No. 1 records, but when John walks on that stage
the rest of 'em might as well leave.

It has been a tough year for the Cash family. June Carter Cash, Johnny's mate and spirited stage partner, passed away on May 15, and now Johnny.

In the September 22 edition of *Time* magazine, it is written:

...if some felt shock at the news of Cash's passing,
they could segue into celebration over a difficult
life made exemplary, an outlaw redeemed by
a woman's devotion. Besides, if you believe,
the Man in Black is now garbed in white, and
the doting husband has eternity to spend with
his beloved.

So it is with heartfelt sincerity that we convey to John Carter Cash, the son of Johnny and June, and to the extended Cash family, our deepest sympathy at this time of great loss.

—Thursday, September 25, 2003

Tributes

The Late Right Honourable
Robert L. Stanfield, P.C., Q.C.

Honourable senators, I rise today to speak to the memory of the Right Honourable Robert Lorne Stanfield.

Robert Stanfield was born on April 11, 1914, in Truro, Nova Scotia. His parents were Frank and Emma Stanfield. His dad was a dedicated public servant who himself was elected to the provincial legislature of Nova Scotia four times, as well as serving as Lieutenant-Governor of our province.

Robert Stanfield began his political career in 1948 when he was elected Leader of the Progressive Conservative Party of Nova Scotia. He was subsequently elected to the House of Assembly in 1949 and re-elected in the general elections of 1953, 1956, 1960, 1963 and 1967. When he took over the Progressive Conservative Party, it had no seats in the legislature. He led the party to power, serving 11 years as our premier. During that time, he also served as Minister of Education.

I attended Queen Elizabeth High School in Halifax where his daughter Sarah was a classmate of mine. While walking to school along Robie Street, one often encountered Mr. Stanfield walking to work. He was always cordial to the young people. He would turn right on University Avenue or Spring Garden Road and head downtown toward his office at Province House.

Mr. Stanfield perhaps enjoyed his best years as a politician in Nova Scotia. His contributions to the province, at a time when the economic outlook was anything but bright, included leaving our province with an industrial base, something which had, until that time, passed by Nova Scotia.

As Minister of Education, Premier Stanfield also left a lasting legacy. The education system was improved through offering Nova Scotia's students not only a better quality of education but also a better rounded one, serving the needs of all students.

Nearer to my heart, Robert Stanfield initiated the first provincial transfers to universities in Nova Scotia. He also initiated a program whereby the province would pay up to 90 per cent of the costs of university buildings, a great contribution to education and to the future of our province.

Mr. Stanfield's home at the very south end of Robie Street was called "The Oaks." Appropriately enough, it is now owned by an education institution, St. Mary's University, and houses my *alma mater*'s Department of International Activities.

In 1967, Mr. Stanfield left Nova Scotia and contested the leadership of the federal Progressive Conservative Party at its convention. He was successful in this, as he defeated Duff Roblin on the strength of a dramatic fifth ballot victory.

Robert Stanfield's days in Ottawa were not as successful as those in Nova Scotia. The moment of ultimate national success narrowly missed his grasp.

It has been mentioned many times that Robert Stanfield might have been a more successful politician if he had been less considerate of other people and their opinions. I do not know what that says about other politicians, but I do know what it says about Mr. Stanfield. He was a person of outstanding quality who harboured strong personal values and was a man dedicated to his family, his province and his country. His family has my deepest sympathy.

—Wednesday, February 11, 2004

Junior Women's Curling Championship

Congratulations to Winning Nova Scotia Team

Honourable senators, I rise today to offer my congratulations to the Nova Scotia team who captured the Canadian Junior Women's Curling Championship this past Sunday, February 15, in Victoria, British Columbia, in a dramatic, come-from-behind, 6-3 victory over the talented Marie-Christine Cantin team from Quebec. The Nova Scotia rink of the Chedabucto Curling Club in Boylston, Guysborough County, Nova Scotia, will now go on to represent Canada at the World Junior Curling Championships.

The new Canadian champions are: Skip, Jill Mouzar of Liverpool; Third, Paige Mattie of Boylston; Second, Blisse Comstock and her sister Chloe Comstock, Lead, both of Lunenburg.

Jill works in Halifax, Paige attends McGill University, Blisse attends Acadia University and Chloe attends St. Mary's University. It is a testament to their dedication, energy and sacrifice that these young women have been able to come together and achieve this high level of championship teamwork.

I am certain that all senators join with me in offering their congratulations to the Nova Scotia team and wishing them every success as the representative of Canada at the World Junior Curling Championships to be held March 20-28 next, at Trois-Rivières, Quebec.

—Tuesday, February 17, 2004

Curling

Nova Scotia—Congratulations to Winning Teams

Honourable senators, I rise with great pride today to inform this chamber of the recent achievements by Canada's curlers on the national and international levels. It truly has been a month of success, not only for the country but for the province of Nova Scotia, as all these tournaments have involved rinks representing my home province.

On February 29, in Red Deer, Alberta, the defending Canadian champions representing the Mayflower Curling Club of Halifax defeated a younger but very talented Quebec rink 7-4, in a very close match at the Scott Tournament of Hearts. The Canadian champions — skip Colleen Jones, third Kim Kelly, second Mary-Anne Arsenault and lead Nancy Delahunt — have won four straight times and a phenomenal fifth championship in six years, both national records.

These dedicated women have learned how to win. They do not rest on their laurels but continue to push themselves to that championship level of their game. The Jones rink is an inspirational role model for all athletes, female and male alike. The Canadian champions will compete in the World Women's Curling Championship in Gavle, Sweden, from April 17 to 25.

On March 14, at the Nokia Brier in Saskatoon, Saskatchewan, another Nova Scotia rink, again from the Mayflower Curling Club of Halifax, bested the defending Canadian champion, Randy Ferbey of Alberta, in a come-from-behind 10-9 victory. The Nova Scotia rink consisted of skip Kevin Dacey, third Bruce Lohnes, second Rob Harris, lead Andrew Gibson and fifth Matt Harris. These men managed to keep up with the Joneses, and they will represent Canada at the World Men's Curling Championship in Gavle.

Finally, over this past week, the Women's World Junior Curling Championship took place in Trois-Rivières, Quebec. As I mentioned in a past statement, the Canadian champions hail from Chedabucto Curling Club in Boylston, Nova Scotia, and did the country proud. Skipped by Jill Mouzar, third Paige Mattie, second Blisse Comstock and lead Chloe Comstock, their record was 10 wins and one loss throughout the tournament. Their only loss was in the final game to Norway by a score of 9-6. That result earned a silver medal for Canada, something of which our junior women champions can be very proud.

I am most pleased today to offer these three tremendous rinks from Nova Scotia this chamber's appreciation for their excellent efforts, and to wish the Jones and Dacey rinks good luck at the World's next month.

—Thursday, April 1, 2004

Curling

World Championships in Gavle, Sweden— Congratulations to Women's Gold Medal and Men's Bronze Medal Winners

Honourable senators, on April 1, I informed you of the national success achieved by three Nova Scotian curling teams and extended good wishes to two of them. Those two were the Colleen Jones rink and the Mark Dacey rink, both of the Mayflower Curling Club in Halifax, both of whom were representing Canada in the World Curling Championships at Gavle, Sweden.

I am delighted to report that the rink skipped by Colleen Jones won its second world women's title with an 8-4 victory over Norway on Saturday, April 24. We congratulate Colleen and her team of Kim Kelly, third; Mary Ann Arsenault, second; Nancy Delahunt, lead; Mary Sue Radford, spare; and Ken Bagnell, coach.

We also congratulate Mark and his team of Bruce Lohnes, third; Rob Harris, second; Andrew Gibson, lead; and Matthew Harris, spare. This talented rink won the men's bronze medal with a 9-3 victory over Norway on Sunday, April 25. It should be noted that the Dacey rink had a perfect 10-0 record in the round robin section of this championship.

We salute these two rinks for their accomplishments, and we thank them for the honours that they have brought to Canada.

—Tuesday, May 11, 2004

Tributes

The Late Honourable Calvin Woodrow Ruck, C.M.

Honourable senators, I am most honoured to rise today to pay tribute to the late Honourable Calvin Woodrow Ruck, who served Nova Scotia with distinction in this chamber and who recently passed away at his retirement home in Ottawa.

I wish to be associated with the remarks of Senators Austin and Oliver. Last Saturday afternoon, Senator Oliver, my friend Graham Downey, the first Black alderman elected in the City of Halifax, and I attended the church service in celebration of the life of Senator Ruck. No less than five clergymen and clergy-women spoke about this honourable gentleman. They all spoke of his dedication to his loving family, his commitment to improving the lot of our Black citizens, especially the young members of the Black community, and the respectful way in which he conducted himself in the service of others.

I should like to share with senators two anecdotes further to those mentioned by my colleagues. Both are testaments to the soulful motivation and high quality of Senator Ruck's work.

As mentioned by Senator Austin, Senator Ruck wrote two books about the history of Canada's Black Battalion, No. 2 Construction, which he called "Canada's best-kept military secret." One Wednesday at National Liberal Caucus — I ask that partisans indulge me this one little indiscretion — Senator Ruck took the microphone and through the chair he asked Prime Minister Chrétien to cause markers to be placed at the unmarked graves of Black veterans who served Canada. In his respectful way, he assured the Prime Minister that he did possess the power to address this situation and that it was the right and respectful thing to do. That Gandhi-like approach by Senator Ruck moved our Prime Minister to direct the minister responsible to confer immediately with the good senator in an anteroom and to fulfil his request. Those markers were put in place forthwith, thanks to that intervention by Senator Ruck.

Senator Ruck was a devote Christian. At his going home celebration his son, Douglas, shared the following story with the host of family and friends gathered. Two uniformed police officers, one Black and one White, came to Douglas' residence in the company of the funeral home staff to receive the senator's remains. As he was laid to rest in the vehicle, both officers stood alongside, came to attention and snapped a salute. That gesture was a moment of discrimination-free respect, the paramount thing that motivated Senator Ruck in all of his work.

Sometimes, honourable senators, we do not realize the giant qualities of the men and women with whom we associate on a day-to-day basis.

We extend our deepest sympathy to the late Senator Ruck's spouse, Joyce, their sons, Douglas and Martin, and his brother, Arthur, and we thank them for sharing this outstanding man with us.

—Thursday, October 28, 2004

Tributes

The Honourable Richard H. Kroft, C.M.

Honourable senators, I wish to join colleagues in speaking in tribute to the Honourable Richard Kroft, who was my seatmate for nearly all of his six years in this place. I have known Richard for over 20 years. During that period we have collaborated on many fronts, and we became very good friends.

As has been mentioned, Richard distinguished himself in the service of Canada in his chairmanships of our Standing Committee on Internal Economy, Budgets and Administration and the Standing Senate Committee on Banking, Trade and Commerce. Perhaps his greatest contribution has been his talent to get colleagues together to canvass issues of the day over a meal somewhere off Parliament Hill. I shall personally miss that fellowship, Richard, and our many issue-solving sessions.

Since coming to the Senate, his administrative assistant has been Ms. Lisa Fisher. I know that Richard would wish me to record his appreciation and thanks to Lisa for her assistance. I am delighted to report that I am the beneficiary of that period of mutual tutelage as Ms. Fisher now works with me.

Richard, I have always found most interesting your many advices to me regarding your beloved hometown of Winnipeg, including the people and the events of national significance rooted there and which continue to emanate therefrom. However, despite those impressive facts, Richard, I still am not convinced that Winnipeg really should be the capital of Canada.

I wish you, Hillaine, and your family the very best of health and happiness in the years ahead, and I hope that your leisure time will permit you to come to Atlantic Canada to our fabulous, historic coast where our great country began.

—*Wednesday, November 17, 2004*

The Late Sherman Fenwick Homer Zwicker

Honourable senators, I rise today to make a statement on behalf of my friend Sherman Fenwick Homer Zwicker, who passed away on November 9. A proud son of Lunenburg, Nova Scotia, Sherman served as mayor of his historic hometown from 1971 to 1979. He had earlier served for eight years as a town councillor. Over the years, Sherman served on more than 30 volunteer organizations, often as chair, at the town, county, provincial and national levels. He truly led by example.

From 1960, he was president of Zwicker and Company Limited, the family firm that traded in salt fish in the British and Foreign West Indies and South America trades. Prior to retiring in 1990, Sherman served for 10 years as the executive director of the Union of Nova Scotia Municipalities, his most cherished level of governing.

Sherman was the ideal candidate for every political party at the provincial and federal levels. Despite the many courtships, he chose to keep himself true to municipal government by not aligning himself with any party. However, he often reminded me of his willingness to serve in this august chamber and that he was ready to take that call. What a fine senator he would have been.

Early in October, Sherman was recognized for his exemplary community service when he was awarded the Order of Nova Scotia by Her Honour, Lieutenant Governor Myra Freeman. In continuation of the Zwicker family tradition of public service, Sherman saw his son, Peter, elected to Lunenburg's town council on November 16. A devout Anglican, Sherman's committal service was held in St. John's Anglican Church, our partially restored place of worship that he loved so much.

We express our deepest sympathy to Sherman's wife, Barbara, and his children, Peter, Lisa and Andrea, and we thank them for sharing him with us.

—Wednesday, November 17, 2004

Sir Samuel Cunard

Honourable senators, I rise today to make a statement in recognition of Sir Samuel Cunard, whose two hundred seventeenth birthday was celebrated on November 21 last.

Born in 1787 in the family home off Brunswick Street in Halifax, Samuel Cunard is arguably one of the greatest entrepreneurs ever produced by Nova Scotia or Canada. His spectacular business career spanned over half a century. During this time, S. Cunard & Company became a household name in Halifax, and it endures to this day.

At 52 years of age, he gained international acclaim as the "colonial" who successfully introduced steam to the North Atlantic, when in 1839 he founded the incomparable Cunard Line. Samuel Cunard revolutionized ocean transportation, commerce and communication between the old and new worlds.

On May 28, 2004, Canada Post Corporation issued a stamp to commemorate Samuel Cunard. Launched in Halifax, this stamp recognized the risks and successes of Cunard, including his establishment of the Transatlantic Mail Service between England and Halifax in 1840.

The name Cunard is proudly emblazoned on the world's newest and greatest ocean liner, *Queen Mary 2*. This luxury liner is the proud replica of the original Cunard liner that frequently visited Halifax, particularly during World War II when she was converted for wartime service and transported more than half a million service men and women. After that war, the *Queen Mary* brought 50,000 war brides to Pier 21 in Halifax and to their new country, Canada.

Samuel Cunard was a visionary who proved that if you set your sights high and work hard, all is possible. It is, therefore, about time for Cunard to be more fully celebrated by the raising of a statue to him on Halifax's harbourside. We commend the efforts of the Cunard Steamship Society, of Halifax, and its tireless chairman, John G. Langley, Q.C. I thank him for his assistance herein, and I encourage him to continue to work toward the raising of a statue in honour of Samuel Cunard, perhaps on Sir Sam's two-hundred twentieth birthday in 2007.

—Thursday, December 2, 2004

The Honourable Joseph Howe

Tribute on Occasion of Two Hundredth Anniversary of Birth

Honorable senators, I rise to pay tribute to the Honourable Joseph Howe on this, the occasion of the two hundredth anniversary of his birth. He is perhaps the most famous son of my province, Nova Scotia, and a truly great Canadian.

Born in Halifax in 1804 to John Howe and Mary Edes Howe, Joseph Howe made his first mark on our country in 1828 as the publisher of *The Novascotian*. Howe had the goal of not only reporting on the politics of Nova Scotia at the time but also of enlightening his fellow citizens and educate them as to the benefits of achieving responsible government.

Eventually, Howe's writings culminated in a seditious libel suit against himself and *The Novascotian* in 1835. As John Ralston Saul wrote: "His six hour defence and subsequent acquittal is a defining moment of the arrival of freedom of speech in Canada."

In 1835, like the rest of the colonies at the time, Nova Scotia had a real democratic deficit, to use a more modern term, and Joseph Howe fomented the call for democracy. He did this through the promotion of public education, which, to his mind, was the only way to achieve a truly democratic society. Howe believed that every child in Nova Scotia should have the opportunity to learn to read and write, to have access to books, and that every adult who did not have that chance should be afforded the same.

Howe began his official public service in 1836 when he won a seat on the Legislative Council on a platform of support for responsible government. In 1848, after 20 years of toiling, Howe paved the way for the election of the Reformers and the ultimate achievement of responsible government, the first colony to achieve this. As Howe himself put it, this came about without "...a blow struck or a pane of glass broken."

Joseph Howe fought against entrance of Nova Scotia into the Confederation of Canada. He did so on the grounds that it was not a great deal for his home province and that it was being done in an undemocratic manner. Of course, he ultimately lost the struggle but went on to serve this country in the federal cabinet and eventually held the office of Lieutenant-Governor of Nova Scotia for one month before his death in 1873 at Government House.

I wish to salute the Honourable Joseph Howe and to recognize his historic contributions — freedom of speech, responsible government and public education. Our country and my province owe this man a great debt of gratitude. I am humbled to occupy the same office that he once did.

In closing, I wish to recognize with sincere appreciation the efforts of Michael Bawtree, Executive Director of the Joseph Howe Initiative, and to commend that entity for the numerous events it has organized and participated in over this year, all in celebration of the two hundredth anniversary of the birth of Joseph Howe.

—Monday, December 13, 2004

The Late Latham B. Jensen, O.C.

Honourable senators, I rise today to pay tribute to Commander Latham B. Jenson, late of Queensland, Nova Scotia, who was affectionately known as "Yogi" to his naval colleagues and many friends. When he crossed the bar on December 29 last, Commander Jenson left behind a wonderful legacy of service to Canada.

Born in Calgary, he was captivated by the sea and the idea of a career on the navy and enlisted in 1939 at 18 years of age. He served on HMS *Renown*, *Matabele* and *Hood*. On September 13, 1942, then Sub-Lieutenant Jenson was the 21-year-old gunnery and signals officer onboard HMCS *Ottawa* when she was torpedoed and sunk while on convoy escort duty in the North Atlantic. He and 68 shipmates were rescued by a British corvette after five hours in the water; sadly, 138 officers and men were lost. He then served in HMCS *Niagara*, *Long Branch* and *Algonquin*, the first ship to shell the shore defences on Juno Beach in Normandy on June 6, 1944. Following the war he served as an instructor at Royal Roads, where he taught future admirals and senior naval officers. Later he commanded HMCS *Crusader*, *Micmac* and *Fort Erie*, and the 7th Escort Squadron.

In 1964 he retired from the navy, swallowed the anchor and settled in Queensland. He turned his hand to his superb talents as an artist and writer. Among his seven books are *Vanishing Halifax*, *Nova Scotia Sketchbook*, *Fishermen of Nova Scotia*, the autobiography *Tin Hats, Oilskins and Seaboots*, and the limited edition portfolio *Last of the Tall Schooners*. His book titled *Saga of the Great Fishing Schooners* is "the" reference on how to rig a schooner and "the" guide for those wishing to build a model of *Bluenose II*. He illustrated nine other books.

While volunteering as Vice-President of the Heritage Trust of Nova Scotia, Yogi Jenson campaigned tirelessly and successfully to stop the demolition of historic buildings on the waterfront of Halifax. During his community service as Chairman of the Advisory Council of the Maritime Museum of the Atlantic, he led the acquisition of HMCS *Sackville*, the last remaining corvette from World War II, as a memorial to those who fought and won the Battle of the Atlantic.

Commander Jenson was awarded the Order of Canada in 2004 in recognition of his gallant services to Canada, both in wartime and peacetime.

We extend our deepest sympathy to Commander Jenson's wife, Alma, and their children, daughter Sarah and sons Lynn and Tom. We thank them for sharing this valiant sailor, artist, writer and community volunteer with us.

—*Wednesday, February 2, 2005*

Funding of Post-Secondary Education

Adoption of Resolution by Liberal Party

Honourable senators, I rise today to inform this chamber of very recent developments in a subject dear to my heart and dear to the hearts of others present here today as well. Our efforts to propose changes to the manner in which the federal government accounts for and disburses funding for post-secondary education has been advanced. On March 4, 2005, the Liberal Party of Canada adopted as party policy the following resolution:

(a) THAT the Liberal Party of Canada urge the Federal Government to consider legislation that will ensure stable and predictable funding for post-secondary education; and

(b) THAT the Liberal Party of Canada urge the Federal Government to create the Canada Education Transfer (CET), a separate transfer of funds dedicated to post-secondary education; and

(c) THAT the Liberal Party of Canada urge the Federal Government to reach an agreement that prevents provinces and territories from decreasing their own funds for post-secondary education once additional federal funding has been added; and

(d) THAT the Liberal Party of Canada urge the Federal Government to change the funding formula for post-secondary education to provide that per capita funding be granted to the province of the place of learning of the student.

The adoption of this resolution demonstrates once again the manner in which the Liberal Party of Canada has maintained its concern for all members of our society. It understands issues which affect the young people of Canada, and it is able to provide solutions to these problems.

My fellow senators, I must thank the Young Liberals of Canada, Senator Terry Mercer and Michael Savage, a member of the other place and chair of the Liberal Party Post-Secondary and Research Caucus, for their hard work in having this resolution adopted as policy. I also extend my thanks and gratitude to the Canadian Federation of Students, the Canadian Alliance of Student Associations, the Canadian Association of University Teachers and the Association of Universities and Colleges of Canada for their active support in pursuit of this policy.

In closing, I also wish to express my appreciation to the members of this chamber who have spoken out on so many occasions with regard to this very important subject.

—Thursday, March 10, 2005

Tributes

The Late Honourable A. Irvine Barrow

Honourable senators, I rise today to speak in tribute to the Honourable A. Irvine Barrow, who departed this life at Halifax, Nova Scotia, on March 17, 2005, at 92 years of age. Senator Barrow grew up on Tower Road, just three doors north of the Ring family home of my mother, and so I am privileged to be making these remarks today.

The late Senator Barrow served in this place from 1974 until his retirement in 1988. While here, he distinguished himself as Chairman of the Standing Senate Committee on Banking, Trade and Commerce and as Deputy Chairman of the Standing Senate Committee on National Finance, among the other committees on which he served.

Senator Barrow was a career chartered accountant and carried the recognition of his peers as a member of the Fellowship of Chartered Accountants. In 1946, he founded an accounting practice with the late J. C. Nicoll, a firm that grew to have several branches in the Maritime provinces under the Barrow Nicoll & Company banner. He also held numerous corporate directorships and was the pioneer responsible for bringing cable television to the Maritimes, having served as the President of Halifax Cablevision Limited and Chamcook Communications Ltd.

He was a very community-minded person who served as a volunteer President of the Halifax Chamber of Commerce, the Maritime Junior Board of Trade, the Halifax Board of Trade, the Maritime Provinces Board of Trade and the Halifax Commercial Club. His distinguished record also included serving as volunteer President of the Halifax YMCA, Ashburn Golf and Country Club, the Nova Scotia Liberal Association and Chairman of the Budget Committee of Dalhousie University and its successful multi-million dollar capital campaign called "Dalhorizons." He discharged all of these chores with energy, leadership and integrity.

Senator Barrow was a devout member of First Baptist Church and a tireless worker on behalf of it and related religious organizations. In his youth he was a splendid athlete, and he and his late brother, Brock, were awarded medals in a civic ceremony for their heroism in saving a young girl from drowning in the Northwest Arm.

Senator Barrow was predeceased by his wife of 58 years, the former Joyce F. Barnstead, and his brothers J. Brock and Donald F. He is survived by his daughter, Barbara, and his son, Fred, and we convey to them the sincere sympathy of the Senate of Canada upon the passing of this outstanding Haligonian, Nova Scotian and Canadian.

—Wednesday, March 23, 2005

Nova Scotia

Lunenburg—Restoration of St. John's Anglican Church

Honourable senators, on November 6, 2001, I told this chamber about the fire that ravaged historic St. John's Anglican Church in Lunenburg, Nova Scotia, five days earlier. At that time I stated:

> We are prayerful that St. John's will rise again.
> We are confident that her parishioners harbour
> the will and can harvest the resources from across
> Canada to build a replica around those surviving
> pieces of worship.

Honourable senators, I am delighted to report that St. John's has been faithfully restored to its pre-fire beauty. The first service was held in this national historic site this past Sunday at 3 p.m. It was attended by an overflow congregation of parishioners, townsfolk and visitors, all of whom were warmly welcomed by Bishop Fred Hiltz and Reverend Michael Mitchell. At the beginning of the service, the altar was carried into the church and returned to its rightful place by the same six firemen who rescued it from the fire.

This was a most heart-warming event. All marvelled at the detail of the superb work of the craftsmen, tradesmen, shipwrights and artisans. This historic event could not have been realized without the assistance of the Government of Canada, the Province of Nova Scotia, and the Town of Lunenburg, generous friends from across Canada and without, and the devout parishioners of St. John's. We are most appreciative of that support. We are truly grateful for the work of the reconstruction team; all the volunteers, in particular the efforts of the volunteers who led the management of this project; those who led the raising of the funds necessary for this $6.7 million labour of love; and the leadership of the church wardens. Last, but not least, we thank the tireless women, men and youth of the parish and of the neighbouring parishes, who dug through the ashes to recover remnants to be included in the restoration.

Congratulations to one and all. In closing, I urge honourable senators to tour this place of worship during your next visit to Lunenburg.

—Thursday, June 16, 2005

The Honourable John Buchanan, P.C., Q.C.

Honourable senators, I would like to say a few words in tribute to my friend, Senator John M. Buchanan, Q.C. I do not think it was mentioned earlier today that his political career began as an officer of the Liberal Club at Dalhousie University. From there, of course, his hard work led to the office of the premier of our province. While he was there, he was kind enough to give me a certificate of Queen's Counsel, which my family and I deeply appreciated.

Senator Jane Cordy mentioned the travelling back and forth to Ottawa. The seat next to the former premier was always a prime spot among fellow travellers because of the many stories he would share.

I often sat in that seat. I can tell you that upon boarding the plane, Senator Buchanan often greeted the flight crew and asked if any of them knew of his two daughters who served in the industry and of whom he is so very proud. Most of them did. From that strong connection, he would take his seat.

I tell you, everyone getting on that plane heading homeward knew him or he knew them. He had a huge recognition factor and was very kind and courteous to everybody aboard the plane. I often wonder whether or not, John, you were thinking of mounting another run for the premier's office. I think Senator Forrestall mentioned that John never stopped working the bus; nor did he stop working the airplane.

I served with Senator Buchanan for a number of years on the Standing Senate Committee on Legal and Constitutional Affairs. It did not matter what bill we were dealing with, or the nature of it; somewhere and somehow, John Buchanan managed to weave into his remarks a glowing diatribe — call it what you will — usually a heartfelt intervention with respect to Nova Scotia. It did not matter what the nature of the bill was that we had before us. He did so in his own irrepressible style, often trying the patience of the chairs. Nevertheless, he prevailed, we all enjoyed it and some were educated by it.

I shall miss you, John, not only your engaging verbosity, but also your many kindnesses to me and your unabashed expressions of loyalty to Nova Scotia. I wish you and Mavis and your family the very best for the years ahead.

—Thursday, April 6, 2006

Tributes

The Late Honourable J. Michael Forrestall

I too wish to be associated with the remarks of our colleagues here in paying tribute to our friend Senator Mike Forrestall.

My relationship with Michael has been at 35,000 feet or 40,000 feet during our weekly trips back and forth from Nova Scotia to Ottawa. During those time periods, I have often had the opportunity to speak with him and to seek his guidance and advice, political and otherwise.

A few months ago, I spoke to him about the possibility of seeking membership on the Standing Senate Committee on National Security and Defence. It was clear to Senator Mike. He said, "Look, Halifax is a Garrison City and you are from Nova Scotia. You must join us." It was not an order, but it was a pretty firm direction.

Recently, during his hospitalization, I called home and spoke with his brother, Tom, a noted Canadian artist, to check up on Mike. Tom said that he was in to see him the day before in the intensive care unit. Mike was insistent that he had to get out of the hospital, and back to Ottawa: that he had work to do.

I think that anecdote speaks volumes to the undeniable fact that Mike's work for his constituents and the Canadian Forces was underpinned by his strong sense of duty and his steeled commitment to serve his country and his community. We shall miss him. I join my colleagues in extending heartfelt sympathy to his wife, Marilyn, his children, his siblings and his staff.

—*Wednesday, June 21, 2006*

Sail Trainer Of The Year Award

Congratulations to Captain Daniel D. Moreland

Honourable senators, the American Sail Training Association of Newport, Rhode Island, at its annual meeting held last month, bestowed its Sail Trainer of the Year Award upon Captain Daniel D. Moreland, of Lunenburg, Nova Scotia. He is the master of the 300-tonne steel barque *Picton Castle*, which he sailed into her home waters of Lunenburg Harbour this past June to safely complete her fourth around-the-world voyage. The 35 trainees onboard work, stand watch and learn the way of square-rig seafaring, including rigging, sail-making, boat-handling, navigation and practical seamanship.

We salute Captain Moreland for this prized recognition and wish him, the *Picton Castle*, and all who sail in her, fair winds always.

—Tuesday, December 5, 2006

Tribute

Mr. William Gilkerson

Honourable senators, I rise today to pay tribute to William Gilkerson of Martin's River, Lunenburg County, Nova Scotia.

On November 21 last, he was named the winner of the Governor General's Literary Award for Children's Literature (English) for his book, *Pirate's Passage*, which he also illustrated. A sailor, a noted artist, a scrimshander and a writer, Mr. Gilkerson drew upon his many experiences to create a book that the Canada Council for the Arts called "a challenging children's novel with a dangerous edge" and "a work of genius, a benchmark in Canadian literature."

My friend Bill's book also won the New York Library Association "Book of the Season" Award, Young Adult Book Category. Further, there are two competitive offers on his publisher's desk from Hollywood producers who want to make a movie out of *Pirate's Passage*.

We salute William Gilkerson for this well-deserved recognition, and we wish him well as his creative juices continue to flow.

—*Wednesday, December 6, 2006*

Residential School Settlement

Hon. Nick G. Sibbeston: Honourable Senators, I am pleased to provide an update on the residential school settlement. Last May, Canada finalized an agreement with the assembly of First Nations, the churches, and residential schools survivors and their lawyers. The agreement provides a compensation package to everyone who attended an Indian residential school. This payment reflects the damage done to culture, language, individuals, families and communities by this experience. Those students who suffered physical and sexual abuse will receive further compensation through a process outlined in the agreement. The agreement also provides funds for ongoing healing and for a truth commission to communicate the whole story to Canadians.

The agreement had to be approved in full by nine provincial and territorial courts. On January 15, the last court, the Northwest Territories Supreme Court, issued its judgment supporting the settlement. Some of the courts raised issues of concern with some of the details of the agreement and gave only conditional approval as a result. However, in a remarkable and unprecedented move, all judges involved in this case met in Calgary to resolve some of these issues and to agree to a joint sitting of all courts to issue a final approval in the near future.

It is not clear whether this will also resolve the matter of the federal appeal of a single element of the Saskatchewan decision, but one must hope that neither the federal government nor the Saskatchewan court will allow this one issue to hold up the entire settlement. The conclusion of the court process marks a major milestone in a long awaited resolution of this difficult episode in Canada's relations with Aboriginal people.

Once final approval is granted, there will be a five-month period within which all residential school survivors can indicate their objection or agreement. I believe the vast majority will accept the settlement, not because it comes close to compensating them for the abuse they suffered, the loss of language and culture they endured or for the impact that residential schools have had on them as students, their families and their communities, but, rather, they will accept it in the spirit of reconciliation and healing that is so important to their future and well-being.

I know from personal experience the damage that residential schools caused. I spent 11 years in residential schools in the North after being sent away from home when I was five years old. I have cousins and other relatives who were away from their homes and families for 10, 12, 14 years. Imagine sending your child away for those many years; it is a very traumatic experience. I am glad to be able to stand here and say that the matter is finally coming to a conclusion. An agreement has been reached and it is just a matter of the courts approving it.

The agreement is vital to Aboriginal people and to Canada in our ongoing efforts to right the wrongs of the past and to meet our long-standing obligations to Aboriginal people. There is much left to do but this agreement is a shining first step and I commend the Government of Canada, both old and new, for taking the step. In the end, I hope and expect Canada to issue a formal and official apology for what happened to Aboriginal people during the many years that these schools operated. Later, I plan to introduce a motion to enable the Senate to contribute to the reconciliation and healing process. I hope that honourable senators will find it in their hearts to agree with the motion.

—Wednesday, January 31, 2007

The Late Ronald J. Hanson

Honourable senators, on Friday March 23, 2007, the city of Halifax lost one of her most respected and devoted sons, Ronald J. Hanson. Affectionately known as "Butch," he worked for Maritime Tel & Tel for 33 years before retiring in 1990. He was elected alderman for Ward 8 in 1974 and he continued to serve his constituents and city unselfishly until 1999 when he resigned due to illness.

During those 25 years, he also served as deputy mayor and acting mayor of his hometown. A gifted athlete, especially in hockey and baseball, he also gave of his time and personal treasure in coaching minor hockey teams. Perhaps his most cherished task while on city council was his service as one of only two aldermen who sat as founding directors of Halifax Metro Centre. As a lifelong sportsman, he understood the need and value of such a facility. As a forward-thinking councillor, he saw the economic benefit that such a facility would bring to his city.

Ron Hanson was a man of faith, with strong family values and a deep sense of giving back to his community. He and his wife, Sandra, were a real team. We extend to Sandra and their children, Pam, Krista, Ron, Scott and Shawn, our sincere sympathy and we thank them for sharing Butch with us. Ronald Hanson was a lifelong pal of mine, and he will be missed by a host of friends.

—Wednesday, April 18, 2007

Brigadier-General (Ret'd)
Edward A.C. "Ned" Amy

Honourable senators, today, three days after Remembrance Day, I wish to speak about one of Canada's three most decorated military men, Brigadier-General (Retired) Edward A.C. "Ned" Amy, recipient of the Distinguished Service Order, an Officer of the Order of the British Empire, and recipient of the Military Cross, the Canadian Decoration and the American Bronze Star.

Ned Amy was a feisty, fearless tank commander. A 1939 graduate of Royal Military College of Canada, he commanded A Squadron of the Calgary Regiment in Italy, where he won the Military Cross for his "determined and gallant leadership in taking and holding a vital bridgehead over the Moro River" with his Sherman tanks in December, 1943.

He arrived in Normandy, France on July 26, 1944, seven weeks after D-Day. Three days later, then-Major Amy commanded a troop of the 22nd Guard Grenadier Canadian Armoured Regiment in the fight for Grentheville. During the next five weeks, he participated in all the battles that led to the liberation of Normandy. His regiment was awarded four distinctions for its action in the Battle of Falaise. He led an attack against Kurt Meyer's notorious 12th SS Panzer Division that resulted in the liberation of Cintheaux and Bretteville. From August 14 to 17, 1944, his unit was committed to the battle of Rouves, where his tank was destroyed. Finally, he took part in the fights of Falaise against elements of the 3rd SS Panzer Division and the 2nd SS Panzer Grenadier Regiment. After the Battle of Normandy, his unit went into action on the Seine and Somme Rivers, liberating many towns and villages and taking many German prisoners. In the closing months of the war, he fought in Belgium and Germany, where he was wounded. After the war, he remained in the Canadian Forces and retired as a Brigadier-General in 1972.

On July 18, 2007, Olivier Nicholas, Consul-General of France for Atlantic Canada, in a ceremony at Halifax, Nova Scotia, recognized the exemplary service of Ned Amy when he was awarded the prestigious Legion d'honneur, France's highest distinction.

In the citation, Mr. Nicholas stated that Ned Amy "demonstrated outstanding bravery in France during the fiercest battles of World War II."

The award presented to Ned Amy by France was a fitting tribute to a real Canadian hero — a hero in the truest sense of the word.

Until recently, Ned resided at Indian Point, Lunenburg County; he now lives in Halifax, where he is an ardent advocate for the reactivation of the Halifax Rifles as a reconnaissance unit.

I congratulate Brigadier-General Amy, and I thank him and those who served under his command for their service to Canada. I am proud to be his friend.

—*Wednesday, November 14, 2007*

The Late Howard Dill

Honourable senators, I rise today to speak about one of Nova Scotia's best known sons, Howard Dill, who departed this life in his hometown of Windsor on Tuesday, May 20, 2008. Howard was a pre-eminent farmer and a hockey enthusiast.

He developed a most special pumpkin seed, which he labelled the Atlantic Giant. He had the foresight to patent this seed around the world. In 1979, he won the first of many weigh-offs as the international champion grower of the world's largest pumpkins. In the years since, all other champion growers have used his Atlantic Giant seeds. From growing pumpkins for competition, Howard's business grew, as he became the supplier of seeds to many individuals, farms and garden outlets across the globe. Colleagues, no home is as festively decorated with pumpkins and gourds as the Dill residence on College Road during the Halloween season.

The Dill farm includes Long Pond, believed by many to be the location of the first ice hockey game played in Canada. A few years ago, Howard had Long Pond drained, which revealed many old hockey pucks, some made of wood and some of very old rubber all substantiating the likelihood of it being the birthplace of hockey.

Always a gracious host, Howard welcomed all visitors to his farm and was delighted to show them his phenomenal collection of hockey memorabilia.

We all shall miss this legendary man. We thank his spouse, Hilda, and his children, Danny, Andrew, Maureen, Diana and Eddy, for sharing him with us. I am proud to have been his friend.

—*Thursday, May 29, 2008*

Tributes

The Honourable Aurélien Gill

Honourable senators, I wish to be associated with remarks made today in tribute to Senator Aurélien Gill.

Following his appointment to the Senate in 1998, I got to know Senator Gill and to become his friend. Over the years, I have enjoyed his company at social outings, and it was during those gatherings that he schooled me in reserve life and the plight of our Aboriginal brethren.

Since his appointment to the Senate, he has been an ardent advocate for the Aboriginal People, pointing out the shortcomings they are experiencing and urging us to recognize and ameliorate their situation.

One cannot speak of Senator Gill without mentioning his Bill S-234, an act to establish an assembly and an executive council of the Aboriginal Peoples of Canada. Not only is it a solid piece of work, it is the most promising and substantial bill that I have seen initiated during my time in this place. It takes a leader of intelligence, commitment, confidence, passion and bravery to envisage such a bill and to bring it forward.

This far, the Aboriginal people have not done well by the governments of Canada, primarily white folk. It is my hope that this bill of Senator Gill will serve as a blueprint to move forward and to enable our Aboriginal colleagues to have their proper place in Canada and its institutions, as urged by Chief Phil Fontaine last Thursday on the floor of the Senate.

I shall miss the Honourable Senator Chief Aurélien Gill, his friendship and his advice. I wish the best of everything for him and for his family in the years ahead.

—Tuesday, June 17, 2008

The Late Andrew Wyeth

Honourable senators, I rise today to speak about a celebrated American artist, the late Andrew Wyeth, who departed this life on January 16, 2009, at 91 years of age at his home in the village of Chadds Ford, Pennsylvania. He was the fifth child of Carolyn and Newell Convers Wyeth, the illustrator famously known for his work in the books, *Treasure Island*, *Robin Hood*, *The Last of the Mohicans* and *Robinson Crusoe*.

Andrew Wyeth also had a home in the small village of Cushing, Maine, and divided his time between there and Chadds Ford. In both places, he painted his family, friends and neighbours and the rural life that surrounded him, whether the farm settings of Pennsylvania or the maritime settings of Maine.

Andrew Wyeth first exhibited his watercolours in 1936. The following year, he sold out a one-man show in New York. He subsequently began working in egg tempera, and in 1948, he sold his painting *Christina's World* to the Museum of Modern Art in New York for $1,800. That painting has become an American icon, like Grant Wood's *American Gothic* and Whistler's portrait of his mother, and it assured Mr. Wyeth's fame as one of the great artists of the United States of America.

Mr. Wyeth was one of the most popular artists in the history of American art. At the same time, he was targeted by critics. His realist renderings of rugged rural life sparked endless debate about the nature of modern art. Regardless of his critics, Mr. Wyeth painted where he lived. He painted the things that held meaning for him.

In the words of a longtime friend and noted photographer, Peter Ralston, Andrew Wyeth ". . . was incredibly generous, intensely private. He didn't want the world bothering him. Yet nobody loved a good time more than Andy. He could tell stories with the best of them. He was a great, elegant, powerful combination of contrasts."

Andrew Wyeth had a relationship with the Farnsworth Art Museum in Rockland, Maine, that began in 1944. This jewel of the coast of Maine has standing exhibitions of paintings by Mr. Wyeth and his family, and the museum has mounted an exhibition in tribute to him, which is set to open on May 22. If any honourable senators are in the area, I urge them to view that exhibit; it will give your heart a lift.

Mr. Wyeth's earthly remains are buried in a modest seaside cemetery on Hathorn Point in Cushing and next to Christina Olson, the physically challenged lady who was the subject of his iconic painting, *Christina's World*.

We express our deepest sympathy to his wife, Betsy, his sons, Nicholas, and Jamie, who is a renowned painter, and his extended family in Chadds Ford and Cushing.

—Tuesday, March 24, 2009

The Late Senator Edward Moore Kennedy

Honourable senators, I rise today to pay tribute to the late Edward Moore Kennedy, the senior senator from the Commonwealth of Massachusetts, who passed away this past August 25 at his seaside home in Hyannis Port.

Senator Kennedy was born in Boston, Massachusetts, on February 22, 1932, the last of nine children born to Joseph and Rose Kennedy. Needless to say, with such statured older brothers as the late President John F. Kennedy and the late Senator Robert Kennedy, expectations would be high throughout Ted's life. Like all of us, Ted Kennedy had his human foibles, but his service to his country was exemplary and one which was conducted in the public glare.

Earlier in August, when speaking at the funeral mass for his sister, Eunice Mary Kennedy Shriver, he said: "Much is expected of those to whom much has been given."

With his name attached to more than 850 pieces of legislation, one can see that Senator Kennedy achieved much more than may have been expected of him. His ability to seek consensus and work with colleagues across the aisle held America in good stead. He clearly deserved the moniker, "The Lion of the Senate."

Following the slaying of his two brothers, Ted became the central figure of the Kennedy family — the bulwark of faith, optimism, support and perseverance to the widows and children of his brothers, all in addition to that same caring hand that he gave to his own family.

He became a leading light to progressive Americans, often when a cause was in its darkest moments. From speaking out against the war in Vietnam and advocating for a woman's right to choose, to fighting for civil rights, the integration of schools, gun control, same-sex unions, and clean air and water, Senator Kennedy moved America forward. He fought for social justice for all throughout his distinguished career. May Americans embrace his legacy and carry on his dream.

Senator Kennedy was an avid sailor and, with his passing, the tall ships community has lost a real friend. He was a steadfast supporter of tall ships, their sail-training programs and events, often hosting receptions to recruit the visit of the ships, particularly for his home town of Boston. He generously included my home town of Halifax in his solicitations. Over the years, he sailed his own yachts in the coastal waters of Nova Scotia and, near the end, was seen sailing his classic schooner, *Mya*, in the waters of Nantucket Sound.

The issue of health care was there at the beginning of his 47-year career and took on a special prominence at the end. In July 2009, Senator Kennedy challenged those in power to finally realize that dream and, as he put it, ". . . end the disgrace of America as the only major industrialized nation in the world that does not guarantee health care for all of its people." Interestingly, he pointed to Canada's system as a meritorious model.

On behalf of this chamber and the Canada-United States Inter-Parliamentary Group, we extend our deepest sympathy to his wife Victoria, their respective children, and members of the Kennedy family at this time of great loss. To invoke the mariner's version of Psalm 23:

> *Surely sunlight and starlight shall favour him*
> *on the voyage he takes.*
> *And he will rest in the port of God forever.*

> —*Wednesday, September 30, 2009*

Canadian Delegation to Commemorate the Italian Campaign

Honourable senators, during the week commencing November 27, 2009, a delegation of Canadian parliamentarians travelled to Italy to commemorate the sixty-fifth anniversary of the Italian Campaign in World War II. The delegation was ably led by the Honourable Greg Thompson, Minister of Veterans Affairs, who was joined by Senator Meighen and yours truly, as well as by Mr. Guy André, Mr. Rob Oliphant and Mr. Peter Stoffer of the other place.

Most importantly, the delegation included four veterans of the Italian Campaign: Mr. Henry Beaudry, 88 years of age, of the Sweet Grass First Nations Reserve near North Battleford, Saskatchewan; Mrs. Betty Brown, 92 years, of Ottawa, Ontario; Mr. Roland Demers, 87 years, of Tecumseh, Ontario; and Mr. David Morton, 88 years, of Gibsons, British Columbia. They were joined by World War II veteran Robert Ross, 85 years, of Mississauga, Ontario.

Each of these veterans spoke about their own wartime experiences, some publicly, some in private.

Minister Thompson aptly characterized our mission when he said:

> Together, our unique delegation will walk on
> some of the same streets where Canadians fell.
> We will walk among the headstones belonging
> to the youth of another generation. And we will
> remember them by reading their names aloud;
> by running our fingers over letters carved in
> granite, by thinking of dreams unfulfilled, by
> remembering lives lost. And by remembering
> families torn apart by their sacrifice.

One of those graves we visited at Cassino was that of Lieutenant Charles A. Ritcey, of Lunenburg, Nova Scotia. He was the commander of the 11th Independent Machine Gun Company (Princess Louise Fusiliers). He was mortally wounded near the town of Ceprano on May 27, 1944, age 28 years, in the

Battle of Cassino, while acting as a forward observation officer in leading his company. His only concern when he was being treated was for his signaller, Fusilier C.B. Musgrave, of Northwest Margaree, Nova Scotia, who was wounded by the same shell that took Lieutenant's Ritcey's life.

Lieutenant Ritcey was the uncle of my spouse, Jane Adams Ritcey.

Two of the delegation were youth: Nolan Hill from Calgary, Alberta, and Melanie Morin of Drummond, New Brunswick, 16 and 17 years of age, respectively. Each spoke eloquently about a deceased soldier from their respective province whose resting place is known only unto God. These two young people represented the youth of Canada very well, and confirmed our pledge to "remember them."

The delegation also participated in ceremonies of remembrance and laid wreaths at the Price of Peace Monument in Ortona, the Moro River Canadian War Cemetery, the Breaching of the Gothic Line Plaque in Rimini and the Coriano Ridge War Cemetery in Rimini.

The Italian Campaign was one of the bloodiest and costliest for Canada in World War II, where more than 6,000 Canadians died. Of the 16 Victoria Crosses bestowed in World War II, three were awarded to Canadians for their heroic services in the Italian Campaign. We visited the sites where those Canadian heroes earned the Victoria Cross — Major J.K. Mahony in Roccasecca; Captain Paul Triquet in San Martino and Private Ernest Alvia "Smokey" Smith in Cesena. The Italian Campaign has not received the attention of other campaigns but deserves more attention and should be taught to our young people. Perhaps that attention will prompt all Canadians to reflect on the price of freedoms gained, and ensure that we shall keep our pledge to remember those who fell and those who suffered injury.

—Friday, December 11, 2009

Saint Mary's University Huskies

Congratulations on Winning
CIS Men's Hockey Championship

Honourable senators, I rise today to pay tribute to Saint Mary's University of Halifax, Nova Scotia, and its men's varsity hockey team. Yesterday, at Thunder Bay, Ontario, the hockey Huskies defeated the number one ranked Alberta Golden Bears 3-2 in overtime to win the Canadian Interuniversity Sport University Cup as national champions.

This game was an intense struggle between two evenly matched teams. Despite injuries and changes to the lineup, the Huskies worked their way to victory. Although they have experienced numerous near-wins in the past, this was the first national title for the hockey Huskies.

Credit must be given to Saint Mary's head coach, Trevor Stienburg, who led his hard-skating team to victory in our tough Atlantic conference to reach the national playdown. A former Atlantic and Canadian "Coach of the Year," he coached Canada's gold medal winning team in the World University Games at Torino, Italy, in 2007. He is a man of solid personal values who fought back from a severe personal health scare to lead the Huskies this year. We truly appreciate his leadership.

As a Santamarian and former hockey Husky, I am proud of Coach Stienburg and his champion team led by their captain Marc Rancourt and rookie goalie Neil Conway. They all bring credit to Saint Mary's University, to our Atlantic conference and importantly to themselves. I know that former athletic director Bob Hayes, former coach Bob Boucher and mentor Fr. John J. Hennessey, S.J., are smiling down from their perch in the Huskies' skybox. I ask all senators to join me in extending congratulations to this team of champions.

—Monday, March 29, 2010

2010 International Ice Hockey Federation World Women's Under-18 Championship

Congratulations to Canadian Women's Hockey Team

Honourable senators, I rise today to recognize and celebrate Canada's under-18 women's hockey team, which won the gold medal at the International Ice Hockey Federation's World Championship held in Chicago last weekend, with a 5-4 overtime win against the United States of America. This game was the third straight time that Canada and the United States squared off in a gold medal game, with the U.S. winning the first two.

Canada was behind 3-1 after the first period and 4-3 after the second. With only eight minutes left in regulation time, Jenna McParland scored to tie the game for Canada. At the 3:10 mark in overtime, Jessica Campbell, captain of Canada's team, tipped in Brigitte Lacquette's point shot to win the game and the gold medal for Canada.

Ms. Campbell's overtime goal gave her seven goals and 15 points in five games and earned her the Most Valuable Player award for the tournament. Ms. Lacquette finished second in points, with 13. She had a plus-minus of plus 15, and was named the top defenceman.

Jillian Saulnier of Halifax, Nova Scotia, was our team's assistant captain and finished fourth in scoring with four goals and 10 points in five games.

Team Canada was back-stopped by Carmen MacDonald, a 17- year-old goalie from Pictou, Nova Scotia. She made 37 stops in the championship game. MacDonald's .947 save average was tops in the tournament, and she posted a minuscule 1.12 goals against average in three and a half games.

Assistant coach Lisa Jordan, who is also head coach of the Saint Mary's University women's hockey team, said of Ms. MacDonald:

> She made two of these "Wow!" saves during a
> 5-on-3 penalty kill in the third period. It was
> just amazing and it allowed us back in the game

and sent it to overtime. She was a major positive influence in how the game turned out.

Following the game, Dan Church, coach of Canada's team said:

It's historic for us. It's our first win at this age group and we really worked hard to improve the skill level. As most Canada-U.S. games are, it was a true test of the rivalry again and I thought both teams performed really, really well.

It is with much pride that I say to this team of talented, athletic young women, congratulations and well done. Très bien! Go, Canada, go!

—Thursday, April 15, 2010

Tributes

The Honourable Peter A. Stollery

Honourable senators, it is my true pleasure to rise and pay tribute to the Honourable Peter Alan Stollery, world explorer, journalist, taxi driver, businessman, member of Parliament, fisherman, bread maker — and I suspect butcher and candlestick maker, but I have no proof of such — teacher, stove repairman, bibliophile, linguist, roofer and senator — a Renaissance man.

Renaissance men thirst for knowledge. Knowledge, as we know, is power, and Peter Stollery possesses that power to a degree that I have rarely encountered. He did not settle for books as the sole source of his knowledge. His approach to life has been scientific in that he did not only read about the world, he went to experience it, feel it, see it and touch it.

To say that his life experiences have been rich does not begin to scratch the surface of his journeys: riding elephants through Asia, hitchhiking through Europe, driving through North Africa, travelling with the French Foreign Legion, and biking through Russia and Central America — living through life.

It is no surprise then that our former colleague Senator John B. Stewart once remarked of Peter Stollery, "he will make what seems to be an out of left field remark about a certain subject, which over time invariably ends up being true."

Senator Stollery has served this chamber and the other place for 38 years — 38 remarkable years — and he has done so with an élan that probably will never be duplicated.

The office that I occupy is across the hall from that of Senator Stollery. That closeness has enabled me to hear of his exploits and to enjoy his learned insights as we tried to rationalize some of the world's problems. I shall truly miss those conversations.

Of his many works, I must applaud Senator Stollery for his chairmanship of the Standing Senate Committee on Foreign Affairs and International Trade and its Africa Report, surely one of the most important and poignant studies ever undertaken by the Senate of Canada.

I thank you, Senator Stollery, for sharing some of your life with us in this place, and I await news of your future travels. In closing, I refer to the words of the late Senator Harold Connolly:

> Can I praise you who could at once protest you have only done what you have been called upon to do? Would you not argue that the rewards which have come to you in satisfaction of heart and soul, if not in material things, have more than compensated for any services you have given? And yet, I must risk your protest. You have given so much and asked so little that surely you are entitled to know something of the esteem in which you are held. In the hearts of those you have served, there is stored up for you a wealth of gratitude. Voiceless it may be but it is all the more tangible therefore, surpassing far anything that could be inscribed upon a page or built of stone or marble. I remind you of this because it is your due.

Bon voyage, Mr. Chairman.

—*Tuesday, November 23, 2010*

Tributes

The Late Honourable Norman K. Atkins

Honourable senators, I wish to be associated with remarks made by so many honourable senators here this afternoon. Senator Norman Kempton Atkins was a steadfast Canadian and a consummate senator. He always strove for the good of Canada, seeking the common ground and reaching across the aisle when that was deemed to be the wise thing to do.

As Senator Ogilvie mentioned, there was his devotion to Acadia University — the blue, white and garnet that he played for, bled for and constantly supported. How I savoured my hearty discussions and conversations with him about the rivalry between his Axemen at Acadia and my Huskies at Saint Mary's University.

I shall miss him. I shall miss the dinners we enjoyed at his and Mary's home, his wisdom, his advice and his friendship. My thoughts go out to his family members, the boys and Mary. I shall miss him very much. I miss him now.

I remember when Senator Cowan, Senator Munson and I went to an Acadia University event about two or three years ago when they inducted Norman into their special hall of fame. The tributes that filled that night were absolutely deserved and he was so proud of that university and his work with it — with the School of Business and on the board. Many schools would be well served to have an alumnus like Norman Atkins.

—*Tuesday, December 7, 2010*

The Late Madison Rae McDougall Burch

Public Cord Blood Bank

Honourable senators, I rise today to speak about a young friend of mine, Madison Rae McDougall Burch, who departed this life on Friday, February 11, a month before her fourth birthday, at home in Marriotts Cove, Lunenburg County, Nova Scotia, surrounded by family and friends.

In August 2009, Madi was diagnosed with acute myeloid leukemia. She immediately began chemotherapy at the Izaak Walton Killam Health Centre in Halifax. Full remission was achieved, but Madi relapsed quickly. She was transferred to The Hospital for Sick Children in Toronto for a bone marrow transplant. This time the remission held longer, but, in November 2010, the cancer returned permanently.

Honourable senators, during her much-too-short life, Madi redefined the meaning of courage and taught us all the power of spirit, determination and joy. In her final months she lived every day to the fullest. She became an avid reader and, through the kindness of the Children's Wish Foundation, Madi and her family travelled to Walt Disney World in Florida, where her beloved Tinker Bell welcomed her. Madi inspired countless parents to hug their children even tighter every day, and she left everyone with wonderful, lifelong smiles and memories.

Honourable senators, Madi inspired many doctors and scientists to work harder to solve cancer's mystery. It is in this regard that we must not let this precious, short life pass without meaning and contribution. The Hospital for Sick Children, who lovingly cared for Madi while she was their patient, is conducting leading research in the field of stem cells and regenerative medicine. Stem cells are the body's building blocks or master cells that can develop or differentiate into any type of tissue or organ. These cells are the focus of regenerative medicine, medicine that involves growing new cells, tissues and organs to repair, replace or regenerate those damaged by aging, disease or injury.

Stem cells have been collected post-birth without controversy from umbilical cord blood and from bone marrow. Canada would benefit from the availability of umbilical cord blood, reflecting the genetic diversity of Canada, and which could be used to provide matched recipients with stem cell therapies.

However, Canada is the only one of the 58 developed nations in the world without a public cord blood bank. In addition to that scientific shortcoming, not having a cord blood bank is expensive. In 2010, Canada imported 90 units of cord blood at a cost of between $40,000 and $80,000 each, totalling an average cost of $5.4 million.

I do not know if the availability of matched umbilical cord blood would have helped Madi or saved her, but I do know that we should do all we can to have such blood available for children like Madi and the thousands of other Canadian children suffering from myeloid leukemia and other diseases.

In Madi's name, I urge the Government of Canada to establish forthwith a public cord blood bank.

—*Thursday, February 17, 2011*

Political Cynicism

Honourable senators, I am moved to make a statement today about a matter of national significance, that being the attitude of cynicism that prevails in our population regarding their participation in and opinion of the politics of Canada.

On Wednesday, June 8, Prime Minister Harper and his entourage flew to Boston to watch a hockey game between the Bruins and the Vancouver Canucks. That junket was made in a publicly-owned aircraft at a cost to taxpayers of some $57,000. It took place on the same day that Mr. Harper and his government announced thousands of job cuts, and it took place a short 20 days after Mr. Harper and his government were sworn into office. His arrogance did not take long to surface. It was an untimely and insensitive waste.

That money could have seen two Canadian families who are down on their luck through for a year. It is little wonder that only one-in-four eligible voters voted to support Mr. Harper and his program. It is little wonder that only a little over 60 per cent of Canadians eligible to vote cast their ballots. It is little wonder that Canadians, including our youth, are cynical. It is little wonder that our youth are crying out for equity and accountability among those in authority. It is little wonder that our youth, such as Brigette DePape, are moved to take unusual actions to protest such arrogant and wasteful actions by this Conservative government. Canadians truly do deserve better.

—*Wednesday, June 15, 2011*

Hunger Count 2011

Food Banks Usage in Canada

Honourable senators, I rise today to mark the release of HungerCount, the annual report from Food Banks Canada, and to bring your attention to a growing problem in Canada.

March 2011 saw the second highest usage of food banks in this country since 2008. In fact, food banks usage has risen 26 per cent since 2008. Each month in Canada, 851,000 people find themselves having to access a food bank. Honourable senators, 322,000 of this total are children. Forty-seven per cent of that 851,000 are women. Twenty-four per cent identified themselves as First Nations, Metis or Inuit. Almost 20 per cent were immigrants. Five per cent were seniors.

Honourable senators, 12 per cent of those using food banks are actually working but cannot afford food for their families. Over 90,000 Canadians visit food banks for the first time each month. This is a disgraceful situation, which cries out for attention.

In my own province of Nova Scotia, 22,000 people sought assistance from food banks. Fully one third were children, and that represents an increase of 32 per cent in total use since 2010 in Nova Scotia.

Food Banks Canada recommends three main means of reducing the need for food banks in Canada. First, invest in affordable housing so that Canadians do not have to choose between paying rent and feeding their families. Second, modernize employment insurance to better support older workers who have lost their permanent jobs. Third, create federally led programs to ensure that Canadian jobs are well-paying jobs.

Honourable senators, in light of these concerning numbers, I would ask the government to move to alleviate the pressure on Canadian families who can no longer provide the food their families need.

After all, Canada is one of the wealthiest nations on Earth. We should, as a society, provide the basics for our citizens so that they may have the dignity of providing for themselves and their families.

—Tuesday, November 1, 2011

The Honourable
Celine Hervieux-Payette, P.C.

Congratulations on Receiving the
World of Difference Award

Honourable senators, I rise today to pay tribute to our colleague Senator Céline Hervieux-Payette, on the occasion of her being recognized by The International Alliance for Women for her contributions to the advancement of women.

This recognition came in the form of the TIAW's World of Difference Award, which was presented to Senator Hervieux-Payette last Thursday in Washington, D.C.

In this chamber we all know of our colleague's great dedication to the advancement of women in Canada and abroad, and it is truly gratifying to see her efforts recognized in such a manner, by such an organization.

Let me quote from The International Alliance for Women's citation regarding Senator Hervieux-Payette's worthiness as a recipient:

> When it comes to women's economic advancement,
> there could be few champions stronger or more
> dedicated than Senator Céline Hervieux-Payette
> of Canada. Leading by example in her own career,
> she has blazed a trail for many to follow.

Senator Hervieux-Payette is a true model to young Canadian women, having achieved success in business and success in politics, being elected as a member of the other place in 1979, re-elected in 1980, sworn to the Privy Council in 1983, and in this chamber since 1995, where she became the first woman to hold the title of Leader of the Opposition in the Senate. She is a dedicated contributor as Deputy Chair of the Standing Senate Committee on Banking, Trade and Commerce, and is highly regarded for her volunteer work with the Financial Women of Quebec and Women at the Top.

Senator Hervieux-Payette, in a world where women still fight for equality at the best of times — and in some places for so much less than that — let me leave you with a call to arms from Clare Boothe Luce, an American politician and writer:

> Because I am a woman, I must make unusual
> efforts to succeed. If I fail, no one will say,
> "She doesn't have what it takes." They will say,
> "Women don't have what it takes."

I know, sénatrice, that you will continue to prove women do have what it takes, no matter what it takes.

Féliciations, chère collègue!

—Wednesday, November 2, 2011

Maurice Guitton

Congratulations on Recognition by Aerospace Industries Association of Canada

Honourable senators, on Wednesday, November 2 last, the Aerospace Industries Association of Canada, the AIAC, held its fiftieth anniversary gala reception and dinner in Ottawa. The AIAC is not-for-profit organization that advocates on aerospace policy issues that have a direct impact on aerospace companies and aerospace jobs in Canada. Indeed, it is "the" national voice of Canada's aerospace industry.

In 2009, the AIAC established the James C. Floyd Award, which honours Mr. Floyd, the chief designer for Avro Canada, who played a central role in the development of some of the greatest planes ever produced in Canada, including the C-102 Jetliner, the CF-100 fighter and the Avro Arrow. This award is presented annually by the AIAC to visionaries whose contributions have made a difference in the industry.

At its recent gala, the AIAC presented its James C. Floyd Award to Maurice Guitton of Lunenburg, Nova Scotia, whose corporate path is truly an inspirational story of leadership, entrepreneurship and devotion. He founded Composites Atlantic Limited in Lunenburg in 1993, and it has become a leader in the design, testing, certification and manufacture of advanced composites for the aerospace, space, defence and commercial industries. He created a successful business, beginning with a staff of 8 and rising to its current 320 employees.

Mr. Guitton has revolutionized the aerospace industry, in particular helping small- and medium-sized enterprises upgrade their quality assurance standards to meet the industry's requirements, and he has driven the development of new technologies to help improve the quality of produced parts. Among the items of advanced composites that Composites Atlantic designs and manufactures are the struts that hold the engines to the wings of Boeing's new "787 Dreamliner" ultra-light jetliner.

He was one of the initiators of the Aerospace and Defence Industries Association of Nova Scotia, where he served as president and a director, as well as assisting in the creation of other aerospace associations in Atlantic Canada.

We therefore congratulate Maurice Guitton for this most deserved recognition bestowed upon him. He truly is a Canadian aerospace visionary and I am proud to call him my friend.

—Tuesday, November 15, 2011

Mr. Fred George

Congratulations on Honorary Doctorate

Honourable senators, on Sunday, October 23, 2011, Saint Mary's University of Halifax, Nova Scotia, held its fall convocation. Among the degree recipients at that ceremony was Mr. Fred George, of Bedford, Nova Scotia, upon who was conferred a Doctor of Commerce *Honoris Causa*.

Mr. George's career path is quite remarkable and most inspiring. He left his civil war-torn country of Lebanon and arrived in Nova Scotia at 19 years of age. He began operating a video business and then was a supplier of bottled water to Walmart, Superstore and Sobeys.

In 1997, he co-founded Gammon Gold Incorporated. As its president and chairman, he transformed that small exploration company into one of the largest gold and silver producers in Mexico. He presided over the listing of the company on the stock exchanges of Toronto, New York, American and Berlin. Under his leadership, the market capitalization of Gammon Gold, recently renamed AuRico Gold, grew from $2 million to $2.4 billion in just five years. There are a number of millionaires walking around Nova Scotia today thanks to the vision and tenacity of Mr. George.

Mr. George, on behalf of Gammon Gold, has been the recipient of a number of awards, including the Best Producing and Active Exploration Company in Mexico, as well as the best performing gold and silver company in the world for 2003 and the first six months of 2004, as rated by Mineweb. In 2006, Mr. George was the recipient of the first-ever Community Development Model Award, bestowed by the Governor of Chihuahua, Mr. Jose Reyes, in recognition of Gammon Gold's support of the community and the creation of over 1,000 direct jobs and 6,000 indirect jobs. He was granted honorary Mexican citizenship for his contribution to that country's mining industry and economy. He is considered an expert in Canadian-Mexican relations.

He is known for his infectious energy and his ability to motivate others. He is a frequent speaker at the Sobey School of Business at Saint Mary's University. He extols that there are three kinds of people: those who make it happen; those who watch it happen; and those who ask: What happened? He is clearly of the first kind, proclaiming that he is delighted to be the single largest taxpayer in Nova Scotia.

Mr. George is also committed to making a difference in the lives of others. He founded the Fred George Foundation, which supports many community organizations and causes, including education, autism, mental health and learning disabilities; and he serves as an adviser to the President William Clinton Foundation.

He is a staunch supporter of the Royal Canadian Navy and our military families. In recognition of that work, on November 4, 2011, Mr. George was appointed an honorary captain in our navy.

Thus, it is with pride and gratitude that we congratulate Doctor Fred George, an outstanding entrepreneur and philanthropist; and I welcome him as a fellow alumnus of Saint Mary's University.

—Wednesday, November 16, 2011

President John F. Kennedy

Forty-eighth Anniversary of Assassination

Honourable senators, 48 years ago today, at 12:30 p.m. Dallas time, or 2:30 p.m. our time — about now, I guess — President John F. Kennedy was assassinated. His passing has haunted us to this day. What the world would have been like had he lived, we can only speculate. He provided light at a time when there seemed to be only darkness. His assassination was such a shock that, as one poet once wrote, since he was "a man so full of life even death was caught off guard."

At that time, I was serving as treasurer of the student council at Saint Mary's University in Halifax. Our executive had a meeting set for 3:45 p.m. The council president, Michael Cox of Lewiston, Maine, walked into our little office and said, "President Kennedy has been shot," whereupon the ceiling light burnt out. I shall never forget that moment.

—Tuesday, November 22, 2011

Tributes

The Honourable Francis Fox

Honorable senators, I wish to be associated with the remarks made by fellow senators here today in regard to our friend Senator Fox.

Senator Carignan mentioned your work with regard to the establishment of Telefilm. That is but one of the great things you have done with respect to the creative people of our society.

Your work and recognition of the writers, the actors, the performing arts and the artists has been exemplary. It has been an absolute pleasure for me to rally behind your leadership as you led us through various issues dealing with that sector of our community, the culture of the creative. Francis, you really understood that group of unsung heroes in our community, who do not really get the credit and support they should get.

I want to thank you for that, and I wish you and your family all the best in the future.

—Wednesday, November 30, 2011

Tributes

The Honourable Tommy Banks

Honourable senators, I wish to be associated with the remarks of my colleagues here today with regard to my seatmate, the Honourable Tommy Banks, who is anything but retiring.

Tommy, I have deepest respect for your high intelligence, your high degree of participation and involvement here in the Senate, your wonderful sense of humour and your generous sharing of your musical talents on behalf of the arts and other community causes.

Without repeating all that has been said here today, whether it has been flying in a Black Hawk helicopter gunship outside the wire in Afghanistan, watching the stage performance of *Guys and Dolls* in London, enjoying your talents as you sang at a friend's piano in Oakland, Lunenburg County, Nova Scotia, or socializing over supper with you and Ida, it has been a gas. I really shall miss you. I wish you, Ida and your family all the best. I will be out to see you in Edmonton. Thank you, Tommy.

—*Tuesday, December 13, 2011*

The Honourable Irwin Cotler, P.C., O.C.

Honourable senators, I rise today to speak to the sad circumstance of a great Canadian, the Honourable Irwin Cotler, member of Parliament for the Liberal riding of Mount Royal in Montreal. I paraphrase from an article which appeared in the *National Post* yesterday by the distinguished journalist and professor, Andrew Cohen.

Moscow, December 1978. In the coldest winter in a century, we gather in our overcoats in a dim corridor of the Hotel Ukrainia; it is safer to meet in the cavernous halls, we reckon, than in our rooms, which are said to be bugged.

We are there to meet Russian Jews desperate to emigrate. The regime has denied them exit visas. They are known as refuseniks.

In our anguished conversation, they mention the name of a Canadian Jew, more than once, with deep reverence. "Do you know Irwin Cotler?" they ask softly. "Have you met him?"

Irwin Cotler was teaching law at McGill University. We all knew him or knew of him as a champion of human rights. It was Cotler who embraced dissidents such as the imprisoned Natan Sharansky and would help free him.

Cotler's commitment to Russian Jews is one of many in a dazzling career as lawyer, teacher, advocate, parliamentarian and cabinet minister. Cotler is an officer of the Order of Canada. He has received nine honorary degrees and a bushel of accolades. By any standard, he is an exemplar of excellence and rectitude.

But this is Canada, a big country with a strange and growing streak of smallness in its politics. And so it is that Irwin Cotler, 71, now faces . . . the Conservative Party and its politics of smear. . . the Conservatives brazenly distributed a flyer to his constituents in 2009 claiming that he had attended "the anti-Semitic" human rights conference in 2001 in Durban, South Africa. Didn't you know that Cotler is a closet anti-Semite?

More recently, the Conservatives have made telephone calls in his riding suggesting that Cotler is planning to retire, which will cause a by-election.

The Speaker in the other place, in an incredibly flawed decision, without reference to numerous parliamentary principles and precedents, ruled yesterday that this did not breach Mr. Cotler's parliamentary privilege. The Speaker declared the action "reprehensible" but, amazingly, could not find a breach of privilege despite the fact that the calls asked for Conservative support in an imminent by-election, which, of course, is a lie — just another lie.

The Conservative Party immediately hid behind freedom of speech, as if freedom of speech was enshrined in our Constitution to provide a refuge for the scoundrels that abuse it. Allowing such practices only furthers the feelings of cynicism and contempt people feel toward politics and politicians. Mr. Cotler, of course, deserves much better, as do all Canadians.

—Wednesday, December 14, 2011

Mr. John Christopher

Congratulations on Retirement

Honourable senators, I rise today to pay tribute to John Christopher of Ottawa, Ontario, who retired on September 1, 2011, having worked with Canadian parliamentarians for 40 years as a research officer and subsequently as an analyst with the Library of Parliament.

Trained as an urban and transportation planner, he assisted Senate and House of Commons committees involved in transportation, including transportation security and safety. As part of his responsibilities, he organized fact-finding trips for committees within Canada, the United States, Europe, Australia and New Zealand. In his capacity as a researcher, he authored reports and papers on such topics as airline restructuring, trucking safety, passenger rail, a national marine strategy and aviation security.

For a number of years he also served as an adviser to the Canada-United States Inter-Parliamentary Group. As a member of that group I had the opportunity to observe John's dedicated work first hand and to benefit from his guidance and support.

On behalf of the Canada-U.S. Inter-Parliamentary Group and the committees that he served, I thank John for all of his professional help. I wish John and his family the best of health and happiness and smooth sailing in the years ahead.

—Thursday, December 15, 2011

Black History Month

Mrs. Evelina Upshaw

Honourable senators, in this Black History Month, I rise to pay tribute to Mrs. Evelina Upshaw of Halifax, Nova Scotia. Born in Windsor Plains, Hants County, Nova Scotia, she was married at 19 years of age and is a mother who brought up her six children as a single parent when her husband left home. She moved to the Mulgrave Park neighbourhood of Halifax 50 years ago. There she raised her family and lifted a Black community through food and prayer, kindness and wisdom.

Despite her humble circumstances, Mrs. Upshaw has fed children who might not otherwise eat. She has spoken out for her Black community and has been a tireless visitor of the sick and dying. She has been a proud member of Cornwallis Street Baptist church for more than 50 years, singing in its choir and volunteering for 33 years in its hot lunch program for kids who were going without food because their parents were at work. For years, Mrs. Upshaw planned and prepared meals herself, cooking for up to 130 kids each morning while her own children were at school. Today, at a youthful 84 years, with her fellow volunteer Liz Jackson, she serves up to 80 brown bag breakfasts each weekday morning to kids in Mulgrave Park.

Mrs. Upshaw also passes out some lessons on behaviour and respect with her food. All children must wash their hands before eating and thank the Lord for the food they receive. She will not allow swearing or fighting, or throwing food or unkind words. She has thousands of kids in her extended family, and decades later those recipients of Mrs. Upshaw's kindness still call her "mom." She continues to try to put young people in the right place.

Affectionately known as the Queen of Mulgrave Park, Mrs. Evelina Upshaw is a true role model for all races, and a real heroine.

—Wednesday, February 15, 2012

Lunenburg Academy

Honourable senators, yesterday marked the last day of classes at the Lunenburg Academy in historic Lunenburg, Nova Scotia. This school was built in 1894-95 on Gallows Hill and is affectionately known as the "Castle on the Hill." The site was chosen following an acrimonious debate in town council. The resulting tie vote was broken by Mayor Watson Oxner casting in favour. He was defeated in the next election.

The school was designed by H.H. Mott of Saint John, New Brunswick, and was constructed by the Oxford Furniture Company of Oxford, Nova Scotia. When that builder exceeded the $35,000 budget, the town council dismissed it and engaged local master carpenter Solomon Morash to finish the building.

The Lunenburg Academy opened its doors on November 7, 1895, and was part of the county academy system of schools in Nova Scotia's Department of Education, teaching grades 1 through 12. The last continuous such house of learning, at its closing yesterday the academy was an elementary school teaching primary through grade 5. Beginning on March 21, 2012, the new Bluenose Academy will open its doors for grades primary through 9.

On March 6, 1984, the Historic Sites and Monuments Board of Canada designated the Lunenburg Academy as a site of both national and architectural significance. In 1995, upon its centennial, the academy was featured on a stamp of Canada.

This remarkable building is a landmark in the town of Lunenburg. Its unusual architectural style is enhanced by an abundance of decorative Victorian designs, sometimes referred to as gingerbread, which create a unique structure admired by townsfolk and visitors alike.

The Lunenburg Academy is owned by the Town of Lunenburg. In 1981 the Lunenburg Academy Foundation was incorporated as a society of volunteers whose mandate is to upkeep, preserve and restore the academy. That community service has been successfully carried out under the caring leadership of Roxanna Smith and Jane Ritcey. It is now the task of the town and that foundation to strive to ensure that the academy space continues to be used for education-related purposes, and we wish them well in that work.

—Thursday, March 8, 2012

Hon. Catherine S. Callbeck

Congratulations on Famous 5 Foundation Honour

Honourable senators, I rise today to pay tribute to our colleague, the Honourable Senator Catherine Callbeck. Yesterday, at a luncheon convened by the Famous 5 Foundation, she was honoured in celebration of her leadership on behalf of women and for being the first elected female premier in the history of Canada.

The moderator of this event was Maureen McTeer, and Senator Callbeck's co-honourees were Deborah Grey, the first Reform Party member elected to the House of Commons; and Audrey McLaughlin, the first female leader of a political party, the NDP, in the House of Commons.

I would like to share with you some of Senator Callbeck's trail-blazing achievements. She was the second woman ever elected to the Legislative Assembly of Prince Edward Island. That was in 1974, as a member for the Fourth District of Prince. She served as the first female Minister of Health and Social Services, Minister Responsible for the Disabled and Minister Responsible for the Non-Status Indians of Prince Edward Island.

She was the first woman elected as the member of the House of Commons to represent the constituency of Malpeque, in 1988. She was elected Leader of the Liberal Party of Prince Edward Island on January 23, 1993, and was sworn in as premier two years later.

She was elected as the member of the First District of Queens in the P.E.I. general election of March 29, 1993, and was thus the first woman to be elected premier in the history of Canada.

She is the recipient of an honourary Doctorate of Laws degree from her *alma mater*, Mount Allison University, in Sackville, New Brunswick. She was named sponsor of HMCS *Charlottetown*. In 1996, she left provincial politics and returned to work in her family's business.

On September 23, 1997, the Right Honourable Jean Chrétien called her to the Senate of Canada.

Since being in the Senate, she has poured herself into the work of numerous committees and the causes of her fellow Islanders and Canadians. Perhaps her work of most longevity and encouragement for women has been the report she produced as co-chair of the Prime Minister's Task Force on Women Entrepreneurs, in 2003.

In 1997, in recognition of her unselfish community service, Senator Callbeck was awarded the Rural Beautification Shaw Award, for her contribution to the enhancement of rural life on her beloved island.

On November 21, 2006, she was named one of Canada's "Top 100 Most Powerful Women" by the Women's Executive Network, and, on June 10, 2008, she was an inaugural inductee into the Canadian Women in Politics Hall of Fame.

In March 2011 she was honoured by Equal Voice as a Trailblazer at its National Recognition reception in Ottawa.

In June 2011 she was inducted into the Junior Achievement Business Hall of Fame of Prince Edward Island.

Senator Callbeck, yours is an extraordinary record of achievement, and you are an exemplary role model for women in Canada.

We are all very proud of you, and we know that you are not finished your leading work. We congratulate you for the most deserved recognition that you received yesterday from the Famous 5 Foundation.

—Wednesday, June 6, 2012

Congratulatory Address to Her Majesty Queen Elizabeth II on Anniversary of Sixty Years of Reign

Message from Commons Concurred In

Honourable senators, my colleague, Senator Day, prepared some remarks, but he had to go to chair the Finance Committee and has asked me to deliver them to the Senate.

As we sweep through the life and times of Queen Elizabeth II, Queen of Canada, we recall 60 years on the throne, 60 years of devoted service to her peoples and her lands, spanning the careers of nine Canadian Prime Ministers. A public figure from the day of her birth, she has been a constant target of universal curiosity throughout her life.

Elizabeth Alexandra Mary of Windsor was born on April 21, 1926, during the political and economic turmoil before World War II. She was crowned Queen at 25 years of age, the same age as her predecessor of the same name, Elizabeth I. She succeeded to the throne on February 6, 1952, during the reconstruction of almost every facet of our society following that war. Her coronation, itself, was on June 2, 1953.

Her Majesty has embraced the new and marvellous invention of television, presided over the reformation of the Commonwealth concept, adjusted, expanded and modified the place of the Crown within its disparate realms, embraced both multiculturalism and technology, and responded stoically to personal family challenges. During the last 60 years, the Crown has evolved with the times, due, in large measure, to her leadership as an exemplary figure of duty, continuity, dignity, goodness and stability in our rapidly changing world.

Elizabeth II is the enduring, living symbol of our unique constitutional evolution and our living link with many centuries of our history. Indeed, on being sworn in as a member of the Senate of Canada, the sole oath that we affirm is allegiance to Her Majesty, so help us God.

One could cite the record of the Queen's service of public duty, but the details would be endless. There are plenty of statistics highlighting the incredible volume of her work, the sheer number of the unveilings, walkabouts, Commonwealth tours, official foreign visits, garden parties, weekly meetings with the British prime minister of the day, attention to endless boxes of cabinet documents, hosting of foreign heads of state, investitures of honours on public officials and military heroes, presentations at ceremonies to recognize exceptional cultural figures, presiding at annual openings of Parliament, attendance at numerous religious anniversaries, listening to expressions of welcome from thousands of mayors and other dignitaries, presiding at the annual Trooping of the Colour, and her solemn presence at cenotaphs honouring the valour of her subjects who gave their lives in war for their Queen and country.

This week, there is a strong sense of nostalgia in Canada. Our newspapers report the reminiscences of many Canadians who recall important moments in our Queen's life of service that relate to our own lives. For so many of us, this week has been an occasion to pause and reflect on our prosperity and good fortune under our Canadian monarchy. I strongly believe we would not be ourselves without the monarchy. The person wearing the crown is at the apex of our society — a pivotal figure above the controversies of our age.

Our laws invoke the Queen's name: Queen Elizabeth II is the ultimate Commander-in-Chief of our Armed Forces and is, therefore, the focal point of our unity as a people. The Queen embodies the ties that bind us together; she is a living symbol of our nationhood. We congratulate Her Majesty on the celebration of the Diamond Jubilee of her reign, and we pray that Queen Elizabeth II, Queen of Canada, may continue to reign in peace and prosperity.

—*Wednesday, June 6, 2012*

The Late Raylene Rankin

Honourable senators, I rise today to pay tribute to Raylene Rankin of the Rankin family of Mabou, Cape Breton. Raylene passed away on Sunday, September 30, after a long and courageous battle with cancer, at the young age of 52 years.

Raylene and her siblings, Cookie, Heather, Jimmy and the late John Morris, formed the great musical group The Rankin Family, who not only achieved success on the charts and sold more than 2 million records, but also began a resurgence of Celtic culture and Gaelic music that continues today.

Indeed, beyond the success of The Rankin Family, Raylene had two albums of her own; the most recent entitled "All the Diamonds," which was released this past June.

Many Nova Scotians, on their travels throughout the world in search of education and work, have heard The Rankin Family on the radio and are reminded of not only their heritage, but also of the family and friends they have left behind. This is a truly special gift for someone who is lonely for home. Raylene was a big part of that.

Raylene was also a lawyer, a community leader, a wife, a mother, a daughter and a sister. She will be sorely missed by all.

I wish to express, on behalf of this chamber, our deepest condolences to her husband Colin, her son Alexander, and the Rankin family.

As Raylene so poignantly sang the lyrics of Leon Dubinsky in her crystal clear soaring voice:

> *We rise again, in the faces of our children*
> *We rise again, in the voices of our song*
> *We rise again, in the waves out on the ocean*
> *And then, we rise again.*

—*Wednesday, October 3, 2012*

The Late Honourable
Herbert O. Sparrow, C.M.

Honourable senators, I wish to be associated with the remarks of my colleagues and to touch on one of the items that Senator St. Germain mentioned. The government bill in respect of the Toronto airport had a little clause in it that, as mentioned, denied due process to the parties and the opportunity to have their case heard under the rule of law. That Liberal bill was defeated by one Liberal vote against; and the voter was Herb Sparrow, a man of deep integrity, who was making sure that Canadians would have due process available to them. I was not here at the time, but I remember reading about the case.

When I came here, I got to know Herb and his fabulous sense of humour. For me, who better was there to go to for advice, to try to emulate and to have as a mentor? He was a mentor to me, and that comical, full and robust relationship continued after he left this place. He was a dear friend and a stalwart Canadian. I shall miss him. I offer my deepest sympathy to his family.

—*Tuesday, October 16, 2012*

Nova Scotia
College of Art and Design University

One Hundred and Twenty-fifth Anniversary

Honourable senators, I rise today to pay tribute to the Nova Scotia College of Art and Design University, commonly referred to as NSCAD, in Halifax, Nova Scotia, which marks its one hundred and twenty-fifth anniversary this year.

NSCAD traces its roots back to October 1887, when Anna Leonowens, motivated by her civilizing genius, opened for classes the Victoria School of Art and Design in the then Union Bank Building on Hollis Street in Halifax. An inspired and vigorous crusader, she led a group of lady friends of the school in raising seed money of $5,000 in 1887 and 1888.

Anna went on to become tutor to the children of King Mongkut of Siam. Her work and her relationship with the king resulted in the making of the film *The King and I* starring the late Yul Brynner, a long-running Broadway play and reprised in 1999 in the film *Anna and the King* starring Jodie Foster.

In 1968, a gallery was established in Anna's name in the historic properties area in downtown Halifax.

Arthur Lismer, later to become one of Canada's legendary Group of Seven artists, was principal of the school from 1916 to 1919. It is he who said, "Art is a vital means of education, a powerful agent in stimulating all those faculties that make for complete living." Interestingly, the school was damaged in the Halifax explosion of December 6, 1917, and Lismer fixed the damaged windows using the glass from prints on loan from the national gallery.

In 1925, the school was renamed the Nova Scotia College of Art. In 1948, its four-year art education program began, and in 1969 it began granting university degrees. In 2003, the college was renamed NSCAD University to better reflect its status as Canada's principal independent university dedicated to the visual arts.

In 2006, I was able to persuade Paul Greenhalgh, then president, and Reverend Laurence Mawhinney, then Mayor of Lunenburg, to join forces to establish the Lunenburg Community Studio Residency Program, where three graduates are provided living and studio space for one year to work on their respective art portfolios. Programs modelled after the one in Lunenburg were opened in 2011 in New Glasgow and Sydney.

In his book entitled *The Last Art College* published earlier this year, Garry Neill Kennedy, president of NSCAD from 1968 to 1978, wrote the following:

If the College was to be truly relevant, it had to focus upon the ideas that had challenged the art world and which had begun to change not only the content of the visual arts but their very definition. . . . The art world was being reshaped and we were determined that our mission as artists and as educators was to be part of that reshaping.

It is clear that NSCAD has met Dr. Kennedy's challenge and that it continues to fulfill its mission with vigour and panache. Many collections and galleries would be void of works of art if it were not for the endeavours created by graduates of and teachers at NSCAD.

Thus, we extend our sincere congratulations to NSCAD, its Acting President, Dr. Dan O'Brien, its governors, faculty, staff, students — one of whom is my daughter, Alexandra — alumni and supporters, and wish it another 125 years at the vanguard as an independent teacher of the visual arts in North America.

—*Thursday, November 8, 2012*

The Late Kenojuak Ashevak, C.C.

Honourable senators, I rise today to pay tribute to Inuit artist Kenojuak Ashevak of Cape Dorset on Baffin Island in Nunavut, who departed this life on Tuesday, January 8, 2013, at the age of 85. Her passing marks the end of an era. She was the last of the Inuit artists born and raised on the land and who began to experiment in art-making at Cape Dorset in the late 1950s. She was clearly one of the most talented of those artists.

Kenojuak's life was anything but easy. She gave birth to seven children and adopted at least seven others. In 1951, she was diagnosed with tuberculosis and sent to a hospital in Quebec City to recuperate, leaving her husband Johnniebo and children behind, some of whom died in her absence. Life would also see her thrice widowed. Such events would have defeated all but the most resilient of human spirits. Her endearing survivor spirit was evident when she said in a 1978 interview:

> I like to make people happy and everything
> happy. I am the light of happiness and I am a
> dancing owl.

In recognition of her talent, she was among the original inductees into the Order of Canada in 1967. In 1982, she was promoted to Companion of the Order of Canada. In 2008, she was bestowed a Governor General's Award in Visual and Media Arts. Kenojuak's limited-edition lithographic print entitled *The Enchanted Owl*, published in 1960, was the image used by Canada Post on the 17-cent stamp in 1980. Her work achieved significant commercial value. One of *The Enchanted Owl* prints sold at auction in 2007 for more than $50,000.

In the late 1950s, she began making art prints in the Cape Dorset lithography studio founded by James and Alma Houston. The studio was a gamble but one that ultimately paid off with my friend, Wallie Brannen of Halifax, Nova Scotia, a NSCAD University graduate, in charge during its inception and through the 1970s. Upon meeting Kenojuak in 1974, he said:

Her quiet charm and guarded interest gave
nothing away. There was no hint of the powerful
images to come from her work in lithography.
Her familiar motif — to so many, the face of Inuit
art — was made more bold by the free use of
brilliant colour.

In a book entitled *Cape Dorset Prints: A Retrospective 50 Years of Printmaking at the Kinngait Studios*, published in 2007, the author, Leslie Boyd Ryan, wife of Terry Ryan, who was the first southerner hired by the Inuit to run their print studio, wrote: "Without Kenojuak, there would have been far less light shining in the print studios of Cape Dorset."

Kenojuak's long-time dealer and friend, Pat Feheley, of Feheley Fine Arts in Toronto, likely said it all when she stated: "She was the star of the Dorset artists, but she was also a national icon transcending Inuit art."

We extend our collective sympathy to the children of Kenojuak, including her daughter Silaqqie, who was her travelling companion and translator, and her multigenerational extended family.

—*Wednesday, February 13, 2013*

The Late Edward William "Billy" Downey

Honourable Senators, I rise today to pay tribute to Edward William "Billy" Downey, native of Halifax, who departed this life on Friday, March 8, 2013. He was the son of the late George Alexander Downey and Leotra Tomlinson Downey. An avid sportsman, Billy was a talented baseball player, boxer and hockey player and a groundbreaking, proud Black businessman.

In his younger years, Billy was the manager of the Vaughan Furriers, a Maritime championship junior baseball team of superb Black and White athletes. He was not only the manager but also the visionary who saw no colour as he put together his team, to which he gave his personal treasure. The team built a strong following and regularly drew upwards of 4,000 fans to the games played on the Halifax Commons. The story of Billy and his team is contained in Frank Mitchell's book, *The Boys of '62*.

Billy is perhaps best known for his love of music and the entertainment business. In the mid-1960s Billy, with one of his brothers, Graham, opened the Arrows Club, first in a house on Creighton Street and then moved to Agricola Street. In 1969, Billy moved his Arrows Club to new, larger premises on Brunswick Street. Billy's cabaret rivalled those in Montreal and New York and all places in between. He brought in such entertainers as Ike & Tina Turner, Sam & Dave and Lotsa Poppa, to name a few. His was the place to be. Persons of all stations in society, the great and the near great, of all colour and political stripes made their way to Billy's club and his warm hospitality. Upon closing the Arrows Club years later, Billy opened a new establishment in 1987 on Gottingen Street, called the Open Circle, where he continued his promotion and staging of local and visiting entertainers.

In the late 1960s, one of the entertainers Billy brought to the Arrows Club was Miriam Makeba, the Grammy Award winning folk singer who was married to Stokely Carmichael, then the leader of the Black Panthers. Stokely told Billy that Miriam would not perform unless the Black patrons sat on one side of the Arrows Club and Whites on the other. Billy's response was that Miriam could not perform in his club under such a condition. In Billy's heart, music had no boundaries. Stokely got that message, and Miriam performed to the delight of all, including Stokely, who sat in the mixed audience. Billy Downey did so much to single-handedly defuse the racial tension that then existed in Halifax.

Last month, Billy Downey received the Queen Elizabeth II Diamond Jubilee Medal in recognition of this unique entrepreneurship and community activism. It was a proud moment for him and his family. I thank my colleague Senator Cowan for nominating Billy for this most deserved award.

Last Saturday, more than 500 people gathered at Emmanuel Baptist Church in Upper Hammonds Plains to celebrate Billy's life. He was predeceased by his wife, Carol. We extend our heartfelt sympathy to Billy's children, his sisters and brothers. He was a unique and well-motivated man. I am proud to have had him as a friend.

—Thursday, March 21, 2013

The Late George Jones

Honourable senators, I rise today to pay tribute to country singer George Glenn Jones, late of Nashville, Tennessee. Born in a homemade house of logs in Saratoga, Texas, on September 12, 1931, he was the youngest of eight children of George Washington Jones and Clara Jones. George was born with a broken arm and a big thirst. He departed this life at Vanderbilt University Medical Center in Nashville last Friday, April 26, 2013, at 81 years of age.

George Jones began singing in church. When he was 11, his father bought him a Gene Autry guitar. He first sang for pay by accident; he had taken the bus to nearby Beaumont, gone to Pearl Street, gotten on a shoeshine stand in front of an arcade and begun to play and sing. People put coins in a cup near his feet, and, after two hours, he had more than $24, enough to feed his family for a week or more in 1942. However, they never saw a cent. He stepped into that arcade and blew it all. That was a portent of George's life until 1982, when, with help, love and strength of his fourth wife, Nancy, he ceased using cocaine and got sober.

In this 1996 autobiography, *I Lived to Tell it All*, George candidly wrote about the troubled journey that was his life: "a journey across a sea of whiskey and a mountain of cocaine, in a vehicle of self-destruction."

He went on the say that he was once dying of terminal restlessness and could never understand how a supposedly good singer could be such a troubled person. He wrote, "My talent, though it brought me fame and fortune, never brought me peace of mind."

Indeed, because of his consuming habits, he would fail to appear for some concerts, earning the nickname "No Show Jones."

Upon his discharge from the Marine Corps in 1954, he cut his first record, an original fittingly called "No Money in This Deal." In 1955, he had his first hit with "Why Baby Why." George has had at least one hit in every decade since. He was a tireless artist, who recorded over 150 albums.

In 1981, he won his first Grammy award for "He Stopped Loving Her Today," a ballad that often appears on surveys as the most popular country song of all time. It won the Country Music Association's Song of the Year Award an unprecedented two years in a row. He won again, In 1999, with "Choices." In 1992 he was elected to the Country Music Hall of Fame and in 2008 was among the artists honoured in Washington at the Kennedy Center.

George last played in Nova Scotia on April 12, 2008. My friend Tom Faulkner and I had a chance to spend some time with George backstage before he raised the roof of the Halifax Metro Centre.

Despite his battles with alcoholism and drug addition, brawls, accidents and close encounters with death, George's expressive baritone voice never left him. As Keith Richards said recently, Geoege's voice "needed neither explanation nor context nor country music fandom to appreciate; you [just] loved the sound of it."

As George Jones said in 1991:

> My fans and real country music fans know I am
> not a phony. I just sing it the way it is and put
> feeling in it if I can and try to live the song.

You were no phony, George. You were the real deal, and we extend our heartfelt sympathy to your spouse, Nancy, and to your extended family. Yes, I wonder — who's gonna fill your shoes?

—Tuesday, April 31, 2013

World Oceans Week

Sargasso Sea

Honourable senators, on the occasion of this being World Oceans Week, I rise to speak about the Sargasso Sea. As you may know, the Sargasso Sea gets its name from the distinctive mats of floating *sargassum* algae or, as Dr. Sylvia Earle, American oceanographer, aquanaut, author and *National Geographic*'s explorer-in-residence calls it, the "Golden Rainforest of the Ocean."

The Sargasso Sea is the world's only non-landlocked body of water, located within the North Atlantic Gyre, bounded on the west by the Gulf Stream, on the north by the North Atlantic current, on the east by the Canary current and on the south by the North Atlantic equatorial current. The area of the Sargasso Sea is more than 4 million square kilometres. Honourable senators, let me tell you about the nature and environment of the Sargasso Sea. It is a sanctuary of biodiversity. It supports a range of endemic species and plays a critical role in supporting the life cycle of a number of threatened and endangered species, such as the porbeagle shark, the American and European eel, as well as billfish and several species of turtle, migratory birds and cetaceans.

The *sargassum* algae mats provide a protective "nursery" for juvenile fish and loggerhead sea turtles. Wahoo, tuna and other pelagic fish forage in and migrate through the sea, as do a number of whale species, notably the sperm whale and the humpback.

The Sargasso Sea is under increasing pressure by countless human uses that threaten both the habitat and species it supports. It is faced with several stressors that threaten the long-term viability and health of its ecosystem, such as oil, bilge and ballast water discharge from ships, concentrations of non- biodegradable plastic waste from ship and land-based sources, negative impacts of fishing, harvesting of the *sargassum* algae for fertilizer and biofuel, seabed mining, climate change and ocean acidification.

Honourable senators may have heard of the Sargasso Sea Alliance, which is a partnership led by the Government of

Bermuda in collaboration with other countries, scientists, international marine conservation groups and private donors. All members of the Sargasso Sea Alliance share a vision of protecting the unique and vulnerable ocean ecosystem of the Sargasso Sea. The mission of the Alliance, which has an office in Washington, D.C., is to ensure legal protection for this ecosystem by having it established as a Marine Protected Area by way of a declaration to be signed by supporting countries and international organizations. This so-called Hamilton Declaration is to be signed in Hamilton, Bermuda, in March 2014.

The 2012 Annual Composite Resolution on the Oceans and the Law of the Sea of the United Nations General Assembly mentioned that it "takes note of the Sargasso Sea Alliance, led by the Government of Bermuda, to raise awareness of the ecological significance of the Sargasso Sea."

In closing, honourable senators, it is my hope that Canada will join in this effort to protect the Sargasso Sea and that Canada will be a signatory to the Hamilton Declaration. I humbly ask all honourable senators to canvass friends and colleagues to ensure that Canada, a tri-sea-bound country, supports the Sargasso Sea protection initiative and becomes a signatory to the Hamilton Declaration.

I encourage all senators to visit the website of the Sargasso Sea Alliance at www.sargassoalliance.org to learn the importance of protecting this precious and unique open ocean ecosystem.

—*Tuesday, June 4, 2013*

The Late Mr. Paul Cellucci

Honourable senators, I also rise to pay tribute to His Excellency A. Paul Cellucci, who departed this life in his hometown of Hudson, Massachusetts, on Saturday, June 8, 2013, after a five-year battle with amyotrophic lateral sclerosis, commonly called Lou Gehrig's disease. He was 65 years of age.

I knew Paul Cellucci. Like so many other people from the Boston States, he was a good friend. Born into a close-knit Italian-American family, he worked his way through school and earned his law degree from Boston College Law School while serving as a member of the Reserve Officers Training Corps, from which he received an honorable discharge in 1978, attaining a captain's rank.

Paul was undefeated in his long political career, which began at age 21 when he was elected to the Hudson charter reform commission and then to the Hudson board of selectmen. In 1976, he was elected a state representative and in 1984 a state senator. In 1990, Paul was elected Lieutenant Governor of the Commonwealth of Massachusetts, and in 1997 he became acting governor. In 1998, Paul was elected governor in his own right.

It has been said that he was the only governor in the past few decades to speak with a distinct Massachusetts accent. Those broad Rs were sometimes so thick you had to cut them with a knife.

On April 17, 2001, Paul was appointed U.S. Ambassador to Canada by President George W. Bush. He was a typically moderate New England Republican, fiscally conservative yet middle-of-the-road on many social issues. Those values carried him well in his career at home and during his service to his country while in Canada. He served as ambassador until 2005, and in 2006 he returned to the practice of law in Boston.

Paul Cellucci was U.S. Ambassador to Canada on 9/11, a critical time in Canada-U.S. relations. He used his keen political skills to build a bridge between the Liberal Canadian government and his president, who was not popular in Canada. Upon those September 11, 2001, attacks, Canadian airports agreed to take in more than 200 airplanes diverted from the United States, and Canadian citizens opened their doors to thousands of stranded passengers and crew. He helped to manage that phenomenal hospitality, and he travelled the breadth and width of Canada to thank people.

We shall all remember Paul co-hosting with then Prime Minister Jean Chrétien the rally on Parliament Hill when more than 100,000 people turned out to show their support for their American neighbours to the south.

He never forgot his roots or his homeland. At times, he was as firm as he needed to be in representing his country. Yet, in his memoir, *Unquiet Diplomacy*, a highlight of his career was that outpouring of support he experienced that day in Ottawa and for which he remained ever grateful.

We thank Paul Cellucci for his service and friendship. We express our respect and heartfelt sympathy to his spouse Janet, and their family at this time of premature great loss.

—Tuesday, June 11, 2013

The Late Frederick E. "Ted" Hood

Honourable senators, I rise today to pay tribute to Frederick E. "Ted" Hood, late of Portsmouth, Rhode Island, who died on June 28, a few days after we recessed for the summer, at 86 years. Ted Hood grew up in Danvers and nearby Marblehead, Massachusetts, and served in the United States Navy during World War II.

In 1955 he founded Hood Sailmakers in the back of Maddie's Bar, that venerable sailors' retreat in Marblehead. Ted was the first sailmaker to weave his own sailcloth, which was stronger than conventional Dacron and far more durable. The dense weave laced with brown thread earned him the endearing moniker "Brown Thread Ted from Marblehead." He later moved the business to the Little Harbour section of that town. By the 1970s, Hood Sailmakers had grown into a worldwide network of service and production lofts, with his sails ubiquitous on winning yachts, including all winners of the America's Cup from 1958 to 1971.

He also founded Hood Yacht Systems, which launched the Gemini grooved headstay for racing, and the Seafurl headsail furler and Stoway in-mast roller reefing systems for cruising yachts — all of which he invented.

Ted built and skippered a successful series of keel and centreboard racing yachts under the name *Robin*. In 1959 his career took off when he won the New York Yacht Club Annual Cruise in his first *Robin*. He did so not only as skipper but as designer, builder and sailmaker. In 1962 and 1964, he repeated the feat with *Nefertiti* in the America's Cup trials. Among Ted's many racing victories were the 1961 and 1971 Marblehead to Halifax Ocean Races, the bi-annual yacht race co-hosted by the Boston Yacht Club of Marblehead and the Royal Nova Scotia Yacht Squadron of Halifax; the Newport to Bermuda Race in 1968; and the Southern Ocean Racing Circuit in 1974. Also in 1974, Ted was skipper of the Sparkman & Stephens designed 12-metre *Courageous* and won the America's Cup, defeating Australia's *Southern Cross* four races to nil.

By the early 1980s, Ted turned his focus from sailmaking to boat design and building. He created a line of sailboats under the

"Little Harbour" name, and built many yachts. Various builders worldwide built over 1,500 yachts of his design. In 1986, Ted moved his business to Portsmouth, transforming an old World War II navy fuel depot into one of the largest yacht service, design, brokerage and building operations on the east coast of North America.

He sold his business in 1999 but continued to work on new yacht designs right up to the last days before he crossed the bar. All who knew him were inspired by his innovative mind, entrepreneurial spirit, creative passion and humility. As Vice Commodore Rives Potts of the New York Yacht Club said:

> Ted Hood lived in a time when specialties were
> not the norm. He was the most forward-thinking,
> the most complete yachtsman of that generation,
> and maybe of generations to come. Nowadays,
> we have guys who are excellent helmsmen, or
> tacticians, or bowmen or are good yacht designers
> or sailmakers. Or maybe a good yard manager.
> Ted Hood was all of those and more.

On behalf of the Canadian yachting community, we extend our heartfelt sympathy to Ted's beloved wife, Susan, their children and grandchildren.

—Thursday, October 17, 2013

The Honourable Terry M. Mercer

Congratulations on Honourary Degree

Honourable senators, I rise today to extend congratulations to our colleague the Honourable Senator Terry Mercer, who received an honorary degree from our *alma mater* Saint Mary's University of Halifax, Nova Scotia, on Friday, October 18.

Senator Mercer graduated from Saint Mary's in 1971 with a Bachelor of Arts degree. Following a stint in sales, he was executive assistant to the Minister of Labour and Housing for the Province of Nova Scotia from 1974 to 1978. That work was followed by various positions with numerous provincial and national charities, which led to his leadership in fundraising for those institutions. His peers recognized his dedication when they elected him chair of the Association of Fundraising Professionals Foundation for Philanthropy in Canada. He is a Certified Fundraising Executive and has lectured extensively in Canada and the United States on modern, ethical fundraising techniques.

He served as National Director of the Liberal Party of Canada from 1995 to 2003. During that period, Prime Minister Jean Chrétien regularly sought Terry's opinions on a range of topics. His strong personal values, forged by his education at Saint Mary's, enabled him to discharge those duties with distinction. In recognition of that leadership and community work, Prime Minister Chrétien appointed him to the Senate of Canada on November 7, 2003.

Senator Mercer has given back to his community, doing yeoman volunteer work for numerous community organizations when they sought out his energy and leadership. One beneficiary of his volunteerism has been Saint Mary's University. His deep personal commitment and work as an alumnus has been exemplary. In recognition of his many achievements and service, Saint Mary's University conferred upon Senator Mercer the degree of Doctor of Civil Law, *Honoris Causa*.

That was a great day for the Mercer family, many of whom were in attendance, including the senator's wife Ellen and their son Michael. I know how proud his parents, the late Bessie and Bob, were as they looked down from the best seats in the house.

Congratulations, Senator Mercer.

—Wednesday, October 30, 2013

The Late
Alexander Colville, P.C., C.C., O.N.S.

Honourable senators, I wish to be associated with the recent remarks of Senator Hubley in tribute to the late Honourable David Alexander "Alex" Colville, renowned Canadian artist, a Privy Councillor, a Companion of the Order of Canada and a Member of the Order of Nova Scotia.

In 1944, Alex joined the army and served as an official Canadian war artist. He recorded the D-Day landings in June 1944, the army's advance in the Netherlands and the havoc wreaked by the Nazis at Bergen-Belsen in Germany. He was the first Canadian to enter that concentration camp when it was liberated. The sight of so many dead humans remained in his consciousness ever after and caused him to "talk a lot about his idea of civilization being this very thin veneer that could be disrupted in the blink of an eye," recalled Tom Smart, author of *Alex Colville: Return.*

Alex's paintings are in many important collections, including the National Gallery of Canada, the Museum of Modern Art in New York, the Centre national d'Art et de Culture Georges Pompidou in Paris and the Art Gallery of Nova Scotia, as well as in numerous private collections. He designed the set of coins celebrating Canada's one hundredth birthday in 1967. It's worthy of note that his painting Man on Verandah sold for $1.29 million in 2010, a record for a work by a living Canadian artist.

In an interview in 1984 about the importance of visual art, Alex said:

> Art says that things actually mean something
> and have some sort of co-ordination. I guess I
> would say that, in an almost literal sense, art is
> encouraging, even if it's terrible stuff. It points to
> significance in the universe rather than banality
> or accident.

Alex gave back to his country and was very much a Wolfville community man, serving in numerous ways, including Chancellor of Acadia University from 1981 to 1991, and a driving force behind the establishment of the Valley Hospice Foundation. In his heartfelt eulogy, Dr. James Perkin, long-time friend, said Alex left behind, along with his paint brushes, three life lessons that he believed and practised: Time lost is lost forever; preparation is always necessary; and ordinary things matter.

He was predeceased by a son, John, and his beloved wife Rhoda, a centrepiece of his life who was often depicted in his paintings. At a tribute to Alex on June 10, 2005, it was she who presented a booklet entitled Rhymes for Alex, all penned by her and one of which reads:

> *I think the best gift I can give*
> *Is a little advice about how to live.*
> *Now, instead of storing up treasures in heaven,*
> *You're getting your kicks from a Super Seven.*
> *But when we get to be eighty-five,*
> *Provided we both are still alive,*
> *If we sell all our worldly goods, we might*
> *Be just as content with a Super Light.*
> *And I would go guiltless to heaven above*
> *And you could come too, as my only love.*

We extend our sincere sympathy to Alex's surviving children, Graham, Charles and Ann, his grandchildren and great grandchildren.

—*Tuesday, November 19, 2013*

President John F. Kennedy

Fiftieth Anniversary of Assassination

Honourable senators, I rise today to pay tribute to the late John Fitzgerald Kennedy, the thirty-fifth President of the United States of America, whose assassination happened 50 years ago tomorrow.

Affectionately known as JFK, he was born on May 29, 1917, the second son of the nine children of Joseph P. Kennedy and Rose Elizabeth Fitzgerald Kennedy. At an early age, he was hampered with congenital back problems that would trouble him all his days and lead to a round of surgeries. Despite that pain, he served his country with honour in World War II as the heroic captain of *PT-109*, a torpedo boat, in the Pacific campaign. He was discharged in 1944.

A Democrat, he was first elected in 1946, at 29 years of age, to represent the 11th Congressional District of Massachusetts in the federal House of Representatives. After serving three terms, he was elected as senator for that state in 1952.

Another member of that class of 1946 was Richard M. Nixon. JFK would later outshine Nixon in the televised debates of the 1960 presidential campaign.

More than 68 million votes were cast, and JFK won that November 8 election by a majority of 118,574 votes, the first Roman Catholic to be elected president and, at age 43, the youngest president ever elected then and still.

His inauguration speech, delivered on January 20, 1961, contained phrases that resonate today:

> Together let us explore the stars, conquer the
> deserts, eradicate disease, tap the ocean depths
> and encourage the arts and commerce.

The ending words of that speech passed into the world's consciousness:

> And so, my fellow Americans: ask not what your
> country can do for you, ask what you can do for
> your country.

In his all-too-short 1,000 days in office, he faced huge issues and inspired a nation. He created the Peace Corps, which saw American youth volunteer to serve overseas. He was saddled with the ill-fated Bay of Pigs invasion of Cuba during his third month in office.

JFK motivated his countrymen with the challenge to send a rocket to the moon in the decade of the 1960s, culminating in Neil Armstrong stepping onto the surface of the moon on July 20, 1969.

In 1961, the Soviets erected a wall dividing Berlin. In a stirring speech on June 26, 1963, at City Hall in West Berlin, JFK confirmed his support for the people of all Berlin with the words:

> All free men, wherever they may live, are citizens
> of Berlin, and, therefore, as a free man, I take
> pride in the words "Ich bin ein Berliner."

In October 1962, JFK was faced with the Cuban Missile Crisis. Sensing a nuclear war, he decreed a naval blockade. His negotiations with Premier Nikita Khrushchev of the U.S.S.R. resulted in the Soviets agreeing to remove all missiles from Cuba and the United States agreeing to remove its missiles from Turkey.

He fought segregation in educational institutions, which led to James Meredith, a black man, being enrolled at the University of Mississippi on October 2, 1962.

On June 10, 1963, JFK made his so-called Peace Speech, calling on the Soviet Union to accept his idea of a peaceful rivalry, not a nuclear one. That speech was pivotal and, on July 25, 1963, the U.S.A., U.S.S.R. and Great Britain signed a nuclear test ban treaty. President Kennedy considered this his greatest achievement.

On October 19, 1960, Martin Luther King, Jr. was arrested at a peaceful sit-in. He was denied bail and sentenced to six months' hard labour. JFK, the candidate, phoned Dr. King's wife, Mrs. Coretta King, offering his help. That event linked the civil rights leader with JFK forever.

On November 21, 1963, he asked his National Security Advisor, Michael Forrestall, to "organize an in-depth study of every possible option we've got in Vietnam, including how to get out of there."

That wonderful presidency of energy and hope came to a tragic end the very next day in Dallas, Texas. One can only wonder what good things for the world might have happened had JFK lived.

Yesterday, President Obama presented this year's Presidential Freedom Medals, created by JFK, the first group of which was to be presented two weeks after his death in 1963. They are awarded to those who make:

> . . . an especially meritorious contribution to . . .
> the security or national interests of the United
> States, or . . . world peace, or . . . cultural or
> other significant public or private endeavours.

John Fitzgerald Kennedy continues to do that to this day.
—Thursday, November 21, 2013

Violence Against Women

Honourable senators, I rise today to speak about "Be the Peace," an initiative to end violence against women and girls in Nova Scotia, particularly in Lunenburg County and surrounding areas.

Unfortunately, my province has the highest rate of sexual assault in Canada, a rate of 40 per 1,000 aged 15 and over. Females, not surprisingly, make up 85 per cent of the victims of sexual assault. Furthermore, Nova Scotia has the lowest rate of charges, prosecution and conviction.

Depressingly, a one-day snapshot of 402 male offenders in Nova Scotia correctional facilities revealed that fully one third of them are in custody for domestic violence. Violence against women and girls affects everyone. The types of violence perpetrated include verbal, physical, emotional and psychological abuse as well as sexual assault.

The impacts of this violence are enormous. The impact trauma from intimate partner violence and/or sexual assault can include post-traumatic stress disorder akin to that experienced by soldiers in conflict zones. There are long-term consequences as well. Victims of this abuse can face years of poverty and insecurity. A study showed that women who have been involved in violent relationships relied on food banks 20 times the rate of average Canadians. Victims of sexual assault can experience long-term mental health impacts resulting in lost education, work and income.

There are direct costs to the economy as well. Justice Canada reported in 2012 that the total cost of intimate partner violence was $7.4 billion. This covers everything from medical care costs, police, legal bills, moving costs, safety measures, child care and counselling, and on and on the story goes.

The Be the Peace initiative is a community-based project to reduce violence against women and girls in Lunenburg, Nova Scotia. Be the Peace engages community partners to develop a coordinated community response to this type of violence. Based on collaborative relationships, the initiative also engages men and boys as being essential partners in the effort to end violence against women and girls.

The people who have joined in this initiative are concerned citizens, members of community groups, government agencies, schools, faith ministries, legal institutions, law enforcement, municipal councils, women's groups and those who work to help those affected by violence.

Be the Peace understands that the issue of violence against women and girls is fraught with stereotypes, misperceptions and judgments. There are institutional, structural and social barriers which conspire to delay results and solutions from being found.

Be the Peace seeks a community-based and collaborative approach which brings us all together to make a difference and end this violent scourge on our society.

—*Monday, December 9, 2013*

Clarence Eugene "Hank" Snow

Honourable senators, I rise today to pay tribute to Clarence Eugene "Hank" Snow, the country music legend who was born in Brooklyn, Queens County, Nova Scotia on May 9, 1914.

The one hundredth anniversary of Hank's birth was marked by events last Friday at the Hank Snow Home Town Museum in Liverpool, Nova Scotia, including the unveiling of a Canada Post stamp in his honour. There was a community breakfast; a concert featuring Reverend Jimmie Rodgers Snow — the son of Hank and Minnie Snow — and Larry Gatlin; the premiere of a biopic of Hank's life; a church service led by Jimmie; and a family picnic at the Hank Snow Playground. The museum used to be the Liverpool Train Station; ironically, a place where young Hank slept in warmth on its benches when he was homeless.

The Hank Snow story is absolutely compelling. It's of a person who overcame abject adversity — poverty, childhood abuse, homelessness and a Grade 5 education — to become a legendary country music singer, songwriter and world-class horse trick-riding showman. His career is testament to the fact that one can achieve his or her dreams with drive, commitment, talent and sheer determination.

As a youth, he worked at whatever he could find. At 12 years of age, he went to sea as a cabin boy in a fishing schooner sailing out of Lunenburg. After his second trip, he bought a guitar and began playing and singing for family and friends. After four years and many scary storms, he came ashore. He went to work for Adams and Knickle, Limited, a venerable fishing company in Lunenburg, where he carried and packed cured and dried fish for shipping.

Hank got his first break in the summer of 1933 when he appeared on CHNS Radio in Halifax, then on the seventh floor of the Lord Nelson Hotel. That led to a contract with RCA Victor in Montreal, and as they say, the rest is history.

Following many years of ups and downs, financial pressures and touring, Hank's perseverance got him to the Grand Ole Opry in Nashville, Tennessee, on January 7, 1950. He was 36 years old.

His number one song "I'm Movin' On" secured him a place on the Opry, to which he was invited back for the next 45 years.

In a career of more than 50 years, his achievements are many. Hank's recording contract of 45 years with RCA Victor is the longest of any artist with one company in the history of recorded music. He recorded 883 single records, 85 of which were on Billboard country charts.

His song "I'm Movin' On" has become a country anthem. It was number one on the charts for 21 weeks, the top 10 for 44 weeks and has been recorded in 36 languages. Hank recorded 120 albums and sold 80 million copies of them.

His community work with abused and neglected children earned him numerous honours. His music earned him entry into seven halls of fame in Canada and the United States of America. In 1994, Hank had bestowed upon him one of his most treasured honours, an honorary Doctor of Letters Degree from Saint Mary's University in Halifax.

Hank passed away on December 20, 1999, at his home in Madison, Tennessee. He was 85. He closed each performance with the words, "Good luck, good health, and may the good Lord always be proud of you." We're sure He's right some proud of you, Hank.

—Tuesday, May 13, 2014

United States of America

His Excellency Bruce A. Heyman

Honourable senators, I, too, would like to welcome His Excellency Bruce Heyman and his spouse Vicki to Canada and to their new jobs. I'd like to be associated with the remarks of my colleague Senator Johnson, particularly with regard to the welcoming of their family with them.

I find it most interesting, Mr. Ambassador, that when you were sworn in on March 26 in the United States as the thirtieth Ambassador to Canada, you did so on a prayer book that you inherited from your granddad who immigrated to the United States from Lithuania. It tells me that you do indeed have a strong sense and appreciation of heritage, family and family values.

Having been an investment banker for many years, during the course of that work your job was to help businesses reach their ultimate potential, and I think that will indeed stand you in good stead as you work in your new job here, which I think you have stated to be economic prosperity for both of our countries.

Aside from all of the issues that you have probably heard about in your many briefings, whether it's Keystone, the Windsor-Detroit bridge, NAFTA or Buy American, one thing I would like you to do if you could, which would help all of us, is convince your colleagues south of the border that hydro is a renewable resource. That would help everybody's prosperity and move us forward.

I welcome you here and I look forward to our working relationship, whether in the Canada-United States Inter-Parliamentary Group or in your official job. Welcome to Canada and bonne chance!

—*Wednesday, June 4, 2014*

The Late Dr. Richard G. Rockefeller

Honourable senators, I rise today to pay tribute to Dr. Richard G. Rockefeller, late of Falmouth, Maine, United States of America, who departed this life last Saturday morning at age 65 years. His tragic death was the result of an airplane crash shortly after departing the Westchester County Airport in the state of New York. The sole occupant in the plane, he was returning home from visiting his father, Mr. David Rockefeller, with whom he had celebrated his ninety-ninth birthday.

Richard was a great-grandson of John D. Rockefeller, co-founder of Standard Oil Company. An unassuming, modest and gracious man, he was a well-motivated philanthropist. A Harvard Medical School graduate, he practised as a local doctor in Maine, and taught medicine in Portland, Maine, from to 1982 to 2000.

He served on the board of the trustees of the Rockefeller Brothers Fund for 23 years from 1989, including seven years as its chair, and he was an advisory trustee at the time of his death.

He served as chairman of the board of advisers for Doctors Without Borders for 21 years, until 2010. Richard helped set up that organization's presence in the United States and worked at securing its funding. He had field assignments with the organization in South America, Africa and Southeast Asia.

Richard was a giant in the conservation of Maine. He was a devoted member of the Maine Coast Heritage Trust for 40 years and served as its chairman. Because of him, many generations will be able to enjoy Maine's coast for years to come.

I had the pleasure of working with Richard on the Sargasso Sea Alliance, the entity he co-founded with his friend David E. Shaw, of Portland.

As Speaker Kinsella knows, I was among the international guests at The Pocantico Center, on the estate of the Rockefeller Brothers Fund in Tarrytown, New York, last November. There I participated in the drafting of the Hamilton Declaration, the document which provides for collaboration of the conservation of the Sargasso Sea, known as the "golden rainforest of the Atlantic

Ocean." Richard made that handsome facility available to the Alliance for that important meeting.

For three years, Richard steered the Alliance along, culminating in the signing of the declaration by a number of nations in Hamilton, Bermuda, this past March and the establishment of a secretariat in Hamilton. I only wish that Canada had been a signatory; perhaps we shall be someday.

His recent work on treatment for veterans who suffer from post-traumatic stress disorder is another example of his commitment to giving back to community.

In closing, I wish to be associated with thoughts of his friend James Fallows who wrote in *The Atlantic* magazine:

> . . . I offer sincerest sympathies to his family
> and friends, and hope that the reputation of
> Richard G. Rockefeller, MD, lives on not for
> the advantages he began with but for the use he
> made of them.

—Thursday, June 19, 2014

Food Banks 2014

Honourable senators, I rise today to note that yesterday marked the annual release of Food Banks Canada's report, HungerCount 2014. This year's report is entitled "Why do we need food banks in a country as rich as Canada?"

Senators, 841,191 Canadians are forced, for any number of circumstances, to turn to food banks every month. This is a 25 per cent increase since 2008. More than one third of those helped by food banks are children. One out of every six households helped by food banks has income from current and recent employment.

Food bank use increased in 6 of our 10 provinces. Forty-three per cent of households accessing support from food banks are single people, that is, persons living alone without children. This sector has seen the greatest rise over the years. In 2001, single Canadians made up 29 per cent of those who accessed food banks. In 2014 this number rose to 43 per cent.

Food bank usage by First Nations, Metis and Inuit is still climbing.

In my own province of Nova Scotia, 20,000 people used a food bank in 2014; 30 per cent were children.

The reality is that since the recession of 2007-08, a large number of Canadians have not recovered from the devastating effects of the economic downturn. With poverty being a main driver of food bank use, Food Banks Canada has several suggestions to relieve some of the problems which perpetuate the cycle of poverty for a great many Canadians. These suggestions are as follows: build affordable housing, reduce food insecurity in the North, fix the broken welfare system, reduce the incidence of child poverty, and provide Canadians with the skills needed for well-paying jobs.

Senators, I thank Food Banks Canada for this report and I applaud the work of those who try to provide nourishment for Canadians who can no longer afford this on their own. I hope we can all work together to break this cycle.

Thank you.

—*Wednesday, November 5, 2014*

The Late Wilfred "Wilf" Arthur Charles

Honourable colleagues, I rise today to pay tribute to Wilf Carter, legendary country and western singer. December 18, 2014, marks the one hundred and tenth anniversary of the birth of Wilfred Arthur Charles Carter at Port Hilford, Guysborough County, Nova Scotia.

His father was a Baptist minister, and the family moved to Canning, Kings County, Nova Scotia, when Wilf was still a child. There he began to sing and yodel. He left home at 15 years of age, worked as a lumberjack while also singing with hobos in boxcars. In 1923 he moved to Calgary, where he worked as a cowboy and made some extra money singing and playing his guitar at dances and events throughout the Canadian Rockies. Wilf made his radio debut in 1930 on CFCN in Calgary. Soon thereafter, he was heard on other local stations and then nationally. His popularity grew, and in 1933 he was in Montreal, where he began his recording career with RCA Victor Bluebird Records. He recorded two songs that he had just written, "My Swiss Moonlight Lullaby" and "The Capture of Albert Johnson," both of which featured his superb yodeling and became best sellers.

In 1935 Wilf Carter moved to New York City, where he performed on radio and in concerts until 1937, when he moved back to Alberta and bought a ranch. While in the U.S.A., he took on the stage name of "Montana Slim" to help enhance his popularity with the American public.

Back in Canada, he continued to perform on American and Canadian radio shows and at concerts until he seriously hurt his back in a car accident in Montana in 1940. He was not able to perform again until 1949 but sustained his popularity with periodic record releases. By 1949, he'd sold 2.5 million albums. That year, he again moved to the United States; and from that base he continued to be a major attraction at live events, touring with his own family show. In 1964 he appeared for the first time at the Calgary Stampede and was among the most requested guests on CBC Television's "The Tommy Hunter Show."

Over the years, Wilf Carter recorded over 40 original albums with RCA Victor, recording the last in 1988. In 1991, at age 86, he made his last concert tour. He retired the following year and passed away in 1996 at Scottsdale, Arizona, at age 91. Wilf Carter was inducted into four halls of fame, including the Nashville Songwriters Hall of Fame. His simple honest sound and yodeling skills continued to attract listeners with each generation. Wilf's recording of "Blue Canadian Rockies" and "You Are My Sunshine" are among his most popular. He truly is a father of Canadian country and western music and paved the way for many artists who followed him in Canada and in the United States.

—*Wednesday, December 10, 2014*

The Late Douglas McNeil

Honourable senators, I rise to pay tribute to Douglas "Dugger" McNeil, late of Halifax, Nova Scotia. Dugger McNeil was an athlete, a community man, a politician, a businessman and above all a family man. He passed away in Halifax on January 18, 2015, at the age of 87 years.

First coming to prominence in Halifax as an outstanding all-around athlete, Dugger starred as a defenceman with the St. Mary's Juniors. He actually put himself through school on a football scholarship. He played in the Montreal Canadiens' organization for four years with the Montreal Royals. His teammates included Dickie Moore, Gerry Plamondon and Jacques Plante.

As he put it, and I quote: "In the original six era of the NHL, with such deep talent, backup players spent their days checking the newspaper to see if a regular was hurt because it was the only way to crack the line-up."

When he returned to Halifax after his stint in Montreal, Dugger was player-coach of the Halifax Atlantics senior team, which won the Alexander Cup twice between 1952 and 1954. It was a team he described as one of the finest clubs ever put together outside the NHL. Dugger was inducted into the Nova Scotia Sport Hall of Fame in 2002.

A solid community man, he was one of the original members of the Centennial Arena Commission, which led to the building of a much-needed ice surface in the west end of Halifax.

In 1960 he was elected to the Nova Scotia Legislature, representing the riding of Halifax West for the Progressive Conservative Party of Nova Scotia, with a majority of 2,666 votes. In 1967 he was re-elected to the newly formed riding of Halifax St. Margarets, with a majority of 1,120 votes.

As a businessman, he owned and ran Dugger's Mens Wear in Halifax for over 40 years. It is in that capacity that I came to understand what a good man he was. A former colleague, the Honourable Brian Tobin, was to speak in Halifax at a community fund-raiser. To make a long story short, the luggage of the future Premier of Newfoundland was lost by the airline. The event was a black tie affair and it was 6:30 on a Saturday night. Stores were closed, of course.

I telephoned Dugger and told him of our predicament. He had just gotten home from work but told us to meet him back at his store, which we did. A tuxedo was promptly produced and the evening saved. Dugger closed shop with our thanks and returned home. It wasn't until later I learned he was returning to resume his own birthday dinner with his family. That's the kind of generous and considerate man he was. On his next visit to Halifax, Brian purchased a suit at Dugger's.

Predeceased by his supportive wife, Marion, I wish to extend the condolences of this chamber to his family: son Ross, daughters Marie and Mary-Anne, brother Jack as well as his seven grandchildren.

—Wednesday, March 11, 2015

Brian MacKay-Lyons

Royal Architectural Institute of Canada— Congratulations on Gold Medal

Honourable senators, I rise today to pay tribute to Brian MacKay-Lyons, a resident of Upper Kingsburg, Lunenburg County, Nova Scotia, upon recently being awarded the Royal Architectural Institute of Canada's Gold Medal.

According to the institute, "This honour is bestowed in recognition of a significant body of work deemed to be a major contribution to Canadian architecture, and having lasting influence on the theory and/or the practice of architecture, either — through demonstrated excellence in design; and/or, excellence in research or education."

Mr. MacKay-Lyons graduated from Dalhousie University with a bachelor's degree in science in 1974, and then degrees in Environmental Design and Architecture from Technical University of Nova Scotia in 1974 and 1976 respectively. In 1982 he earned a Master of Architecture in urban design from the University of California at Los Angeles.

Through study and work abroad in Italy, China and Japan under such leading architects as Charles Moore, Barton Myers and Giancarlo De Carlo, Brian gained a wealth of experience, yet his heart lay at home in Nova Scotia.

He returned home to open his own practice in Halifax in 1985, Brian MacKay-Lyons Architecture Urban Design, which 10 years later became MacKay-Lyons Sweetapple Architects Ltd. His work has garnered much national and international attention. Over the course of his career, he has received over 100 awards, including six Governor General Medals and two American Institute of Architects Honor Awards for Architecture. His work has been recognized in over 300 publications. He remains a professor at Dalhousie University, where he has lectured for 30 years.

Mr. MacKay-Lyons sees a widening gulf between the teaching of architecture and the practice of building, or as he puts it, between the head and the hand.

This led to his creation of the Ghost Lab, an educational program that took place on his family farm at Upper Kingsburg. It was his response to academic shortcomings but also an attempt to revitalize the key ingredient of apprenticeship in the education of an architect. He approaches apprenticeship in the traditional sense of that relationship, with a mentor meant not only to teach but to inspire as well.

The essence of Mr. MacKay-Lyon's approach, in his own words, "has been to make architecture about place — its landscape, climate and material culture." To see his creations along the shoreline of Nova Scotia is to see the physical manifestation of these words. His creations are a part of the land. They do not dominate; they enhance the natural beauty. They belong there.

As one of the jury members for the Royal Architectural Institute of Canada put it, "His work is universally recognized as pure, dignified, poetic and beautiful. His work comes from an intimate connection with his communities." The institute's Gold Medal will be presented to Mr. MacKay-Lyons this summer in Calgary, and we extend the sincere congratulations of the Senate of Canada to him.

—*Thursday, March 26, 2015*

Tributes

The Late Honourable Aurélien Gill

Honourable senators, I also rise today to pay tribute to a very dear former colleague, the Honourable Aurélien Gill, who passed away on January 17, 2015, at the age of 81 years.

Aurélien was a teacher by trade, but he was also a community builder and activist, as demonstrated by his lifelong dedication to advocacy in the interests of Canada's indigenous peoples. He served as chief of the Innu community of Mashteuiatsh from 1975 to 1982, as vice-president of the Quebec Association of Indians from 1973 to 1975, and as chairman of the Atikamekw and Montagnais First Nations from 1975 to 1976. Senator Gill was also a key participant in the founding of the National Indian Brotherhood, now known as the Assembly of First Nations. He was a generous adviser to indigenous peoples in other countries.

Summoned to the Senate by the Right Honourable Jean Chrétien on September 17, 1998, Senator Gill further promoted the cause of Aboriginal peoples through his work on the Standing Senate Committee on Aboriginal Peoples and the Standing Senate Committee on Social Affairs, Science and Technology. Part of this work was the recognition of the fact that the relationship between the Aboriginal peoples and the Crowns of both England and France has been nothing short of disgraceful. Yet, despite the erosion of Aboriginal society over the years and the dependence upon government policy, Senator Gill foresaw that Aboriginal peoples might one day control their own destiny.

Such was the vision of Aurélien Gill when on April 30, 2008, he tabled Bill S-234, An Act to establish an assembly of the aboriginal peoples of Canada and an executive council, to establish a third chamber of Parliament. Recognizing the need to break free from the bonds of the archaic, paternalistic Indian Act and the Department of Indian Affairs, this bill would encourage Canada's Aboriginal peoples to play a greater role not only in their own affairs, but also in those of the country as well. An Aboriginal assembly would provide the voice of the peoples recognized in the Constitution Act, 1982.

In the world of inventors, when a person is the first person to think of a product or process, it's called a "flash of genius." Aurélien Gill had that flash of genius when he conceived of his brilliant system of self-government for the Aboriginal peoples of Canada. Much thought went into that bill, and I encourage fellow senators to read it. It is much more than just food for thought; it is the template for Aboriginal government in Canada. As Senator Gill put it:

> This country will never be complete as long as Aboriginal peoples do not have a place in this political architecture.

He also said:

> How can we be anything less than passionate about this, when this concerns the future of our many children, their education, their health, their environment, their pride, their culture and their identity?

After Aurélien's retirement from the Senate in 2008, we remained in contact. I continue to advocate on behalf of his bill, distributing it to numerous chiefs and speaking about it at opportune times. I thank you, honourable Aurélien, for your work and vision. Meegwetch.

Senator Gill is survived by his wife, Aline; three daughters, Guylaine, Carole and Marie-Claude; and 12 grandchildren and two great-grandchildren. I wish Aline and all of you present to know that it was an honour to serve with Aurélien, who taught me much about life among our Aboriginal peoples. We were good friends. He enriched all our lives, and I thank you for sharing him with us.

—*Wednesday, April 1, 2015*

Tribute

The Late Honourable Pierre Claude Nolin—
Speaker of the Senate

Honourable senators, I, too, wish to speak in tribute of the Honourable Pierre Claude Nolin, Speaker of the Senate of Canada. Our friendship began soon after I came to the Senate, when we spent considerable time together on committee work, particularly the Legal and Constitutional Affairs Committee and National Security and Defence. He always showed up; he was always well prepared. He was engaged in the process. His interventions were learned and his mission was for the greater good and the best interests of Canada.

I should say that he became even more endeared to me when I learned that, like me, he, too, was a devoted Habs fan.

In the Senate Senator Nolin's speeches were always well-founded and well-reasoned. One of my most cherished times in the Senate was a couple of years ago, when Senator Nolin and I debated the provisions of a certain piece of legislation across the aisle, trying to engage and convince colleagues of our respective positions and basically to make the piece of legislation a better document. At that time I truly felt like a senator in the classical sense, and it was he who engendered that decorum. I don't think Pierre Claude ever stopped being a student of the law.

Somebody mentioned earlier today about his work internationally. I don't know if colleagues know this, but a few years ago he was invited to the prestigious U.S. Military Academy at West Point to be the guest speaker and to take the salute as the graduating class paraded past. I assure you that those invitations only go out to leaders of strong character and respect. He certainly was all of that.

As has been said, our late Speaker understood the institutions of Canada's Parliament, especially our Senate, its role and importance in the governing of our beloved country.

His is a most premature passing — just as his leadership was taking root. We shall miss him and what might have been. I extend my sincere sympathy to his family. Adieu, mon ami, adieu.

—Wednesday, April 29, 2015

Abraham Pineo Gesner

Honourable senators, this past Saturday, May 2, marked the 218th anniversary of the birth of Dr. Abraham Gesner, late of Halifax, the forgotten father of the modern petroleum industry. Abraham Gesner was born in 1797 at Cornwallis, Nova Scotia, where his parents, who were loyal to the Crown, settled after the Revolutionary War in the United States.

Gesner's first endeavour in life was to ship horses from Nova Scotia to the West Indies but after surviving two shipwrecks, he decided a change was needed and began experimental farming. This too proved unsuccessful and in return for paying his debts, his father-in-law asked him to become a doctor.

Thus, Gesner attended St. Bartholomew's Hospital and Guy's Hospital in London, England, where he became a doctor and a surgeon. It was there that his interest in mineralogy was born, which would lead to his greatest contribution to modern society. According to his biographer, Loris S. Russell, Gesner settled in Parrsboro, Nova Scotia. While visiting patients, he began to study the geological features of the area. Soon he would publish his first book entitled *Remarks on the Geology and Mineralogy of Nova Scotia*. Based on this study, Gesner was employed by the government of New Brunswick to conduct a geological survey of that province, making him the first government geologist of a British colony.

In 1843, Gesner returned to Nova Scotia to farm and practice medicine, while maintaining his curiosity of mineralogy. It was at this time that Gesner first managed to distill bitumen to produce light oil that could be used for illumination. Gesner called it kerosene. Indeed, in Charlottetown in 1846, he gave a public demonstration of his new lamp oil, the significance of which was missed by many. The key to his work was the process he invented. He distilled and refined bitumen to remove the impurities that made it smoke and smell.

He moved to New York in 1853, intent upon making a go of his new product. By 1854 he gained three U.S. patents and founded the North American Kerosene Gas Light Company on Long Island, New York. By 1857, his company was a success but trouble lay ahead. A combination of competition and a loss of patent to rival companies pushed him to the sidelines. His kerosene company was eventually bought by J. D. Rockefeller's Standard Oil, which later took over Canada's Imperial Oil. He received little recognition and even less compensation for his contributions to the petroleum industry. In 1863, he sold his patents and returned to Halifax, where he was appointed Professor of Natural History at Dalhousie University, a post he held at the time of his death on April 29, 1864.

Loris Russell summed up his life best when he wrote:

> Abraham Gesner was a man who believed that science was good, and that through technology it could make a better world in which to live. If he could come back now and see the great aircraft now propelled over continents and oceans by his kerosene he would be delighted but not surprised.

—Tuesday, May 5, 2015

National Vision Health Month

Honourable senators, I rise today to speak in the month of May, which has been recognized as National Vision Health Month, and to congratulate our former colleague, the Honourable Asha Seth and the Canadian National Institute of the Blind for their hard work in making this important issue known to Canadians.

As many of you may know, the CNIB began in the aftermath of the Halifax Explosion, when over 1,000 people lost their eyesight or suffered eye damage due to flying shattered glass resulting from that December 6, 1917, blast. That event, coupled with the return home to Nova Scotia of many World War I veterans with eye injuries, stirred a group of caring volunteers into action. Their work led to the inclusion of those who suffer from blindness in society and to spreading awareness of the difficulties of the vision-impaired in leading a life alongside those who have healthy vision.

National Vision Health Month seeks to achieve more than understanding the problems faced by blind Canadians. There's also the goal of spreading awareness to those of us with vision that healthy eyesight is not a given. We must constantly strive to maintain the health of our eyes for they not only provide us with sight but also with the warning signs that other health problems are afoot, like diabetes and cardiovascular disease.

Honourable senators, one in seven Canadians will develop a serious eye disease in their lifetime. Many of these diseases can be detected only through a comprehensive eye exam. The older we become, the more the chance of eye problems developing. All this to say: Take care of your vision and have your eyes examined. Visit your optometrist regularly.

National Vision Health Month also recognizes individuals and organizations who champion the cause of healthy eyesight through the Vision Champion Award, which is presented by the Canadian Association of Optometrists. The inaugural winner this May is Pat Davidson, Member of Parliament for Sarnia-Lambton. Ms. Davidson has worked tirelessly to promote and protect the vision of Canadians. Her private member's bill, which brought cosmetic contact lenses under the same regulation as prescription lenses, is only one example of her efforts. Our congratulations go to Ms. Davidson and to all those who work to promote healthy eyesight in Canada.

I dedicate this statement to my recently departed friend and my optometrist, Dr. Thom Lawrence, late of Chester Basin, Nova Scotia.

—Thursday, May 28, 2015

The Late Honourable
Alasdair Graham, P.C.

Honourable senators, I too wish to speak in tribute to the late Honourable B. Alasdair Graham, who was my sponsor when I entered this chamber in 1996. He was born in 1929 in St. Joseph's Hospital in Glace Bay, Cape Breton. His father, Jack, had passed away several months before Al was born. Al grew up in the Glebe House at Immaculate Conception Parish in Dominion where he was raised by his mother Genevieve and his uncle, Father Charlie MacDonald.

Senator Graham grew up, as has been mentioned, in a coal mining community where, as he put it, "The coal culture taught people to look after each other." He would bring this lesson from growing up in that community to both the national and international stages.

He graduated in 1950 from St. Francis Xavier University in Antigonish.

It was at St. FX where Al began his career as a newspaperman, working while a student for *The Xavierian*, the campus newspaper; *The Chronicle Herald*; The Canadian Press; the CBC and then as managing editor for *The Casket*, the Antigonish weekly. He also entered the world of broadcasting, doing the play-by-play for St. FX football, hockey and basketball games.

With a growing family, eventually five boys and five girls, work was necessary as expenses grew. Al noted once that, "It seemed every time Jean and I had another child, I'd have to get another job. It was no secret in Antigonish that I had seven or eight jobs at one time."

He ran in the 1958 federal election in Antigonish, losing in the Diefenbaker sweep. He returned to teaching for a stint before coming to Ottawa in 1965 to work as special assistant to the Minister of Labour, the Honourable Allan J. MacEachen.

In 1966 he returned to broadcasting, moving to London, Ontario, where he became vice-president and general manager of Middlesex Broadcasting.

In 1967, Al Graham was made executive secretary of DEVCO in Sydney, Nova Scotia, where he worked to expand that community's economy beyond solely coal.

In 1972, Al Graham was summoned to this chamber by Pierre Elliott Trudeau, his designation being "Highlands, Nova Scotia." In 1975, he became the President of the Liberal Party of Canada, serving two terms.

In 1979, an approach came from the Nova Scotia Liberals for Senator Graham to run for the premiership of the province after the departure of Gerald Regan. As the story goes, the family decided to have a vote on the matter. The result was a tie. His wife, Jean, no political slouch herself, refused to break the tie. Thus, Al would remain in Ottawa doing his good work here.

The Chrétien cabinet call came as Leader of the Government in the Senate and regional minister for Nova Scotia, where he served with distinction from 1997 to 1999.

Internationally, Senator Graham was an active member of Liberal International from 1977 and served as its vice-president. He also was a member of the National Democratic Institute for International Affairs in Washington, D.C., monitoring elections in numerous growing democracies. He recorded these experiences in his 1996 book, *The Seeds of Freedom: Personal Reflections on the Dawning of Democracy.*

After his retirement from the Senate in 2004, Al continued to serve and contribute to the public good as National Patron and Ambassador for L'Arche Canada, as has been mentioned.

On behalf of this chamber, in which he served Canada with such distinction, I extend to his 10 children, 24 grandchildren and four great-grandchildren our sincere condolences.

I would like to conclude with a quote from Senator Graham, which I think says it all:

> The Senate itself is really what you make of it.
> Public life generally is the same way. There are a lot
> of people who need help, so I am always prepared to
> do that and I find it a pretty exciting life.

Thank you, Senator Graham.

—*Thursday, June 4, 2015*

Sheila Watt-Cloutier, O.C.

Honourable senators, I rise today to pay tribute to Dr. Sheila Watt-Cloutier, who on May 29, 2015, had conferred upon her an Honorary Doctorate of Law degree at the convocation ceremony of the Schulich School of Law at Dalhousie University in Halifax. She is the sister of our colleague Senator Charlie Watt, himself no slouch as an advocate for the Inuit people and their Arctic culture.

This is far from her first honour or award. Dr. Watt-Cloutier was a Nobel Peace Prize nominee in 2007 — that was the year that Al Gore won the prize; she was very close — a recipient of the United Nations Mahbub ul Haq Human Development Award and a recipient of 16 other honorary degrees. She is an Officer of the Order of Canada and was depicted on a Canadian stamp in 2012.

Born in Kuujjuaq, Nunavut, in northern Quebec, Dr. Watt-Cloutier has been a life-long advocate in Canada and internationally for indigenous people, their culture and their environment. She was elected President of the Arctic Council in 1995, re-elected in 1998 and became chair in 2002. It was here she played a crucial role in establishing the Stockholm Convention of 2001, which banned the generation and use of organic pollutants that were contaminating the Arctic food web.

Dr. Watt-Cloutier has also made the ground-breaking connection between human rights and climate change. This connection has been key in furthering the protection of the Arctic environment and, with that, the culture of the people of Canada's North.

In her recently published memoir entitled *The Right to Be Cold*, she writes about her work as an activist for Inuit culture, indigenous rights and the protection of Arctic ecosystems.

In her address to the Dalhousie convocation, Dr. Watt-Cloutier spoke of her education having come full circle, beginning with her early childhood school years in Glace Bay, Nova Scotia, and culminating with this honorary degree in Halifax. Dr. Watt-Cloutier spoke passionately of the Arctic as her university, as our university, and she cautioned the graduates and their families in attendance that it's gradually disappearing as a result of our mishandling of the environment and inaction on climate change. She stressed that we need to be more vigilant in our stewardship of this Arctic university and to work to maintain its natural state, not only for the Inuit, but for all people for generations to come.

On behalf of the Senate of Canada, I extend our sincere congratulations to Dr. Watt-Cloutier and encourage her to continue her struggle for a healthy future for the Arctic.

—Thursday, June 11, 2015

The Honourable Wilfred P. Moore

Congratulations on Induction to Maritime Sport Hall of Fame

Hon. Jane Cordy: Honourable senators, last fall, the Maritime Sport Hall of Fame was established to recognize and preserve the legacies of sports teams and athletes from New Brunswick, Nova Scotia and Prince Edward Island who competed and attained the highest honours on a regional, national or international level of competition.

On June 10 of this year, the inaugural class of athletes and teams was officially inducted into the Maritime Sport Hall of Fame in a ceremony held at the Hall of Fame at the BMO Centre in Bedford, Nova Scotia.

Honourable senators, I would like to congratulate Senator Willie Moore, who was included in the inaugural class of inductees as a member of the 1961-62 Halifax Kingfishers Junior A hockey team.

The Halifax Kingfishers were an independent Junior A team competing at a time when junior hockey was struggling for fans and finances. Junior hockey in the province was at a low point in 1961, and the junior leagues had dwindled to a point where the Kingfishers would pick up games against senior teams, junior-juvenile teams and varsity teams in order to remain competitive. And, honourable senators, competitive they were.

The Maritimes were well represented that year on the Kingfishers team, as their roster included players from around Nova Scotia as well as New Brunswick and Prince Edward Island. They captured the Nova Scotia junior title by defeating the Trenton Scotias and the Maritime Junior Hockey Championship title by defeating the Fredericton Capitals.

The Halifax Kingfishers capped off a very successful 1962 season by playing in the Memorial Cup finals against the Ottawa Montagnards. All four games of the series were played in the Halifax Forum before a packed house each night. Nearly 20,000 fans took in the games. The second game of the series was played on the Saturday, and for the first time in Nova Scotia, a local hockey game was televised across the province. Another good friend of mine, George Croucher of Dartmouth, was a teammate of Senator Moore on this great hockey team.

Although the Kingfishers did not win the Memorial Cup, the team is credited with inspiring the tens of thousands of fans who followed the team with great interest during the Memorial Cup run and sparking a renewed interest in junior hockey in Nova Scotia. That interest has continued through to today. The Maritimes now boasts five Quebec Major Junior Hockey League teams, and in 2013, Halifax finally won that Memorial Cup. Many believe that today's success of junior hockey in the Maritimes can be directly linked to the success of that 1961-62 Halifax Kingfishers team.

Senator Moore, I wish to congratulate you on your induction into the inaugural class of the Maritime Sport Hall of Fame.

—*Wednesday, June 17, 2015*

Émilien Allard

Honourable senators, I rise today to pay tribute to Émilien Allard, the Dominion Carillonneur from 1975 to 1976. Born in Montreal 100 years ago on June 12, Monsieur Allard began his lifelong musical career playing the clarinet in a band in Grand-Mère, Quebec. Moving to Trois-Rivières, he studied piano and music theory with J. Antonio Thompson and Father Joseph Gers-Turcotte.

He earned a licentiate diploma from the Conservatoire national de musique in Montreal where he studied the organ and harmony. From 1946 to 1948, he attended the Beiaardschool in Mechelen, Belgium, where he studied with Staf Nees and Jef van Hoof. Earning a carillonneur diploma in 1948, he went on to the Conservatoire de Paris, studying conducting, orchestration and aesthetics.

In 1949, he was named the carillonneur at the renowned St. Joseph's Oratory in Montreal, where he remained for 20 years. Émilien Allard received many honours during his career, including the International Carillonneur's Prize at Mechelen.

In 1975, he was named Dominion Carillonneur and performed in our Peace Tower until he died a year later, in 1976.

Émilien was recognized by his carillon colleagues as one of the most gifted composers in North America for the instrument. He created more than 50 original works and 700 transcriptions, ranging from expressive religious settings and witty folk song arrangements to innovative abstract compositions.

In addition, over the decades, Radio-Canada broadcast his music for orchestra, piano, band and even animated film scores. He was admired as an outstanding performer as well. Indeed, in an article about St. Joseph's Oratory by Geoffrey Vandeville, Monsieur Allard is depicted as a celebrity in Montreal. He quotes *Le Petit Journal* as writing, "In holiday parades, he knows how to make the crowd sing and dance around a 11-bell carillon towed by a truck."

Although he only served as Dominion Carillonneur in the last two years of his life, his performances on the Peace Tower carillon were remarkable to the audience. Indeed, one Hill manager stopped him in the corridor of Centre Block one day with the request, "Mr. Allard, would you please not play pieces with too much virtuosity at the beginning of the afternoon? . . . Everyone in the office leaves their work and rushes to the windows to hear you better!"

On behalf of the Senate of Canada, we express our sincere thanks to Monsieur Allard and to other former Dominion Carillonneurs — Percival Price, Robert Donnell, Gordon Slater and our current Dominion Carillonneur, Dr. Andrea McCrady — for their superb musical renderings which ring out over Parliament Hill.

—Wednesday, June 18, 2015

Canadian Junior Women's Curling Championship

Congratulations to Team Nova Scotia

Honourable senators, I rise today to recognize and celebrate Team Nova Scotia, winners of the 2016 Canadian Junior Women's Curling Championship held in Stratford, Ontario, over the past weekend, and to thank the hosts for their work in convening this event for our youth.

Our 17-year-old skip, Mary Fay, and her team — third, Kristin Park; second, Karlee Burgess; and lead, Janique LeBlanc — as well as Coach Andrew Atherton from the Chester Curling Club, defeated the Sarah Daniels foursome from British Columbia with a score of 9-5. It was a sweet win for the Fay rink, who came close when they won bronze last year in the championship that was held in Liverpool, Nova Scotia.

Last Wednesday night, they beat out Alberta's Kelsey Sturmay with a 9-3 win. Sunday, Fay's rink was leading 5-2 after four ends, but B.C. tied things up in the seventh. Then Fay drew for two in the eighth to capture the lead for good.

The team will go on to represent Canada at the World Junior Championship in Taarnby, Denmark, March 5 to13, 2016. Prior to the World Juniors, they will be representing Canada at the Youth Winter Olympics next month in Lillehammer, Norway.

We wish the Fay rink every success as they represent Canada in these events.

—Tuesday, February 2, 2016

The Late William Gilkerson

Honourable senators, I rise today to pay tribute to William Gilkerson, late of Martins River, Lunenburg County, Nova Scotia, who departed this life on November 29, 2015, at the age of 79 years.

Born in Chicago, Bill led a most adventurous life. At 16, he travelled to Paris where he studied the great masters as he launched into his artistic calling. He joined the U.S. Marine Corps the next year; upon his honourable discharge, he was decorated as an expert rifleman.

He then moved to San Francisco, where he met his wife, Kerstin and pursued his career as an artist and writer, including as a features editor with the *San Francisco Chronicle*. In the late 1970s, Bill moved his family to Massachusetts. In 1987 he and his family settled in Martins River, and he became a proud Canadian citizen.

Bill was an accomplished artist. He worked as an illustrator, a scrimshander and a marine artist. His works have made their way into many private collections and institutions, including the National Geographic Society and the White House.

Bill also wrote numerous books. In 2006 his novel *Pirate's Passage* won the prestigious Governor General's Literary Award for Children's Literature. The celebrated Canadian actor Donald Sutherland purchased the film rights to this book, which he made into an animated, full-length film that was screened nationally on CBC Television in January 2015 to much acclaim.

Bill was also a musician, a bagpiper, a chess player and a hot-air balloon pilot. He revelled in firing his cannons, and he was a seasoned deep-sea sailor who loved sailing his century-old Swedish cutter, *Elly*, across the waters of Mahone Bay.

William Gilkerson was the quintessential Renaissance man.

We extend our heartfelt sympathy to his wife, Kerstin; daughters, Stephanie and Anna; son, Jack; daughter-in-law, Karen; and grandchildren Elly, Jackson, Signe and Hannah.

My friend Bill will be roundly missed by the tall-ships community, the Tibetan Buddhist community and the brotherhood of the coast.

—*Wednesday, February 3, 2016*

The Late
Alberta "Bertie" Hensel Pew Baker

Honourable senators, I rise today to pay tribute to Dr. Alberta "Bertie" Hensel Pew Baker, late of Chester, Nova Scotia, who passed away on December 6, 2015, at the age of 87 years. Bertie put more into those 87 years than one can imagine; her life should be an aspiration to all. There was not a moment wasted.

Born and raised in Ardmore, Pennsylvania, she excelled at all levels at school, winning many awards for equestrian and academic achievements. Bertie attended Sweet Briar College in Virginia, where she distinguished herself as president of her junior and senior classes. She was a member of its newspaper, *The Brambler*; the choir; the glee club; and the Political Economy and English clubs. As well, she was an excellent field hockey player. Indeed, the field hockey team competed internationally and had the reputation of being the toughest in the state.

Bertie graduated with a bachelor's degree, majoring in political science and nuclear physics.

She married Dr. David W. Baker in 1951 and raised a family of six children in St. Davids, Pennsylvania, where she became an active member in her church, a Sunday school teacher and book fair organizer.

In 1971 the family moved to Chester, Nova Scotia, where Bertie would positively affect the lives of so many in our community. She and David opened a tea room called The Thirsty Thinkers, and they began providing books for the local school, which had no library. She was also a trophy-winning skipper at the tiller of her Chester C-class sloop, Whim.

In 1973, special education classes were cut from the public school system. This left many special-needs individuals with no specialized classes to meet those needs. Bertie had the wonderful idea of creating a facility where mentally and physically challenged people could be welcomed and could experience life with dignity, learning and community living. This facility became Bonny Lea Farm, which was a pioneer undertaking that provided vocational day programs and pre-employment programs. Residential facilities were built which today provide a home for 36 adults, including Bertie's daughter.

Bertie continued her lifelong educational journey as well, earning a Bachelor of Education degree from Saint Mary's University at the age of 57, while going on to undertake a Master's Degree in Psychology at Mount Saint Vincent University. In recognition of her tireless, innovative work on behalf of others, she was the deserved recipient of an Honourary Doctor of Letters degree from Saint Mary's University in 1985.

Bertie bravely challenged those who could not see the worth of an individual or a just cause. Following the philanthropic tradition of her family, Bertie would quietly spend her time helping others, not seeking or needing any recognition or thanks. Indeed there are hundreds of organizations and individuals who have benefited from her generosity. She would sum up her view in a Biblical verse from Luke: "To whom much is given, much is expected."

Bertie was predeceased by her husband, David; and son, David. She is survived by her children Deborah, Rebecca, Bonnie, Joseph and Joanna, as well as grandchildren Jennifer, Jacques, Giovanna, and great grandchild, Ethan.

In extending our sympathy to her family, I would also like to give a resounding thank you on behalf of this chamber to Dr. Alberta "Bertie" Hensel Pew Baker for her life's work in making this world a better place. You shall be missed.

—*Thursday, February 4, 2016*

The Late Graham Leo Downey

Honourable senators, I rise today to participate in Black History Month by paying tribute to Graham Leo Downey Sr., late of Halifax, Nova Scotia, who passed away on September 15, 2015. I first met Graham in the 1950s, when playing minor hockey. As a teenager, he was the manager and coach of a team of young players, exhibiting his generosity and leadership qualities at a young age, a born leader. We were good friends since those early days. Perhaps Graham's greatest achievement in sport was the Vaughan Furriers, a multiracial baseball team he put together, managed and coached. The team was known as the "Boys of '62," and they became the Maritime Junior Champions.

Graham also became a community leader. When he was elected as alderman for Ward 3 in October 1974, he became the first Afro-Nova Scotian ever elected to Halifax City Council. Graham would also serve as deputy mayor from 1978 to 1979. I served on council with him from 1974 to 1980 and can attest that he was a consummate alderman, always available to his constituents regardless of race. He served until the year 2000: an historic record of service, of respect and achievement.

Graham was a community-builder. An editorial in a Halifax newspaper spoke of him as "a builder of great note." More than his elected service, Graham was a builder in the maturing of our city. I think that began when he and his late brother Billy opened the Arrows Club on Agricola Street. In their quiet and steadfast manner, they broke down racial divides and defused some very testy situations in the bumpy 1960s.

Graham Downey had solid personal values. He believed that with good work, good things would happen. He was a positive motivator. He and his wife, Ardith, instilled those values in their family, nieces and nephews, grandchildren and neighbourhood kids, encouraging them all to get an education and become involved in their community.

His niece Terry Downey put it best when referring to his community service:

I became aware of his huge political presence in our community observing pedestrians calling out his name on the streets and drivers honking their horns as they drove past him. There was a lot of respect and acknowledgment from people for his contributions to the people of Halifax.

In recognition of Graham's superb legacy of service, giving and hope, the Alderman Graham Downey Bursary has been established at Saint Mary's University under the direction of his wife, Ardith. It will provide financial assistance of $1,000 annually to an Afro-Nova Scotian student from Halifax County. It is a fitting and lasting testament to Graham's life's work that the education of a young student of his race will be aided under his name.

Graham Downey was the recipient of many honours, including the Dr. W. P. Oliver Hall of Fame recognition, the Queen Elizabeth II Golden Jubilee Medal in 2002 and the Queen Elizabeth II Diamond Jubilee Medal in 2012.

He is survived by Ardith, his six children Carmella, Graham Jr., Pricilla, Gordon, Christopher and Stacy, as well as 13 grandchildren and many nieces and nephews. We extend our heartfelt sympathy to them from the Senate of Canada.

Senators, *this* was a good man. Halifax, Nova Scotia and Canada could all use more Graham Downeys.

—*Thursday, February 25, 2016*

Captain Michael Moreland and
Crew of *Martha Seabury*

Recipients of Arthur B. Hanson Rescue Medal

Honourable senators, I rise today to pay tribute to Captain Michael Moreland and the crew of the schooner *Martha Seabury*, sailing on her maiden voyage out of Lunenburg, Nova Scotia.

At the annual meeting of the American Schooner Association in Mystic, Connecticut, on February 20, 2016, Captain Moreland was presented with the Arthur B. Hanson Rescue Medal by the United States Sailing Association's Safety at Sea Committee. This medal is awarded for bravery on the waterways.

Near dark on September 10, 2012, while transiting Buzzards Bay off the coast of Cape Cod, with winds of 23 miles per hour and seas of three feet, deckhand Allison Phillips spotted a 15-foot capsized sailboat with three people clinging to it and waving for help. Captain Moreland ordered the sails to be dropped and steamed to the stricken sailors. His crew hauled the victims on board; they were suffering from hypothermia, vomiting seawater and barely responsive. The victims were given dry clothing and wrapped in sleeping bags to stabilize their condition.

The U.S. Coast Guard was hailed, and a cutter met the *Martha Seabury* around 10:15 p.m. Captain Moreland decided that the seas were too rough to safely transfer the victims to the cutter, so its medic was transferred to the schooner to attend to the victims. Both vessels headed to the lee of a reef, and in calmer waters the victims were safely transferred to the cutter at 10:40 p.m. and then taken to shore.

On behalf of the Senate of Canada, we recognize the exemplary, life-saving seamanship of the crew of the *Martha Seabury*, and we extend to them our congratulations upon receiving the Arthur B. Hanson Rescue Medal. They are Captain Michael Moreland; Chief Mate Paul Bracken; Billy "Ollie" Campbell, the owner of the vessel; Oliver Cote; Allison Phillips; Dan Rutherford; and Gabe St. Denis.

—Thursday, March 24, 2016

The Senate

David Reeves—Tribute on Retirement

Honourable senators, I rise today to pay tribute to our own David Reeves of the Senate Publications Centre, who retired on February 19, 2016, after 35 years in the public service.

David began his career in the Senate in 1995 as a Text Coordinator, and he became the Publications Coordinator in 1997.

His time at the Senate was marked by meticulous attention to detail and excellent service to individual senators, including myself. David's institutional memory was quite amazing. If asked to find a debate, statement or any sort of extract from the *Debates of the Senate*, no matter how vaguely described, David would have it for you in moments. He was quite a remarkable resource to have had at our disposal.

We all know that working in this place can result in long days and odd hours of work depending on the importance of the debate, and that the record must be kept. There are constant deadlines to meet for delivery of chamber and committee transcripts. David would always be dedicated to meeting these deadlines, often working double shifts to ensure the availability of these transcripts for our use.

We tend to take these talents for granted around here. However, we really do have some truly wonderful employees who go above and beyond the call of duty to make this place function properly. David was definitely one of those.

Sadly, David will spend his retirement cheering for the Ottawa Senators, says me, a devoted Habs fan. Luckily, he will have his extensive collection of blues albums to help him cope with the inevitable disappointments.

Sincerely, David is looking forward to spending more time with his nieces, Rachel and Stephanie, and nephews, Graham and Martin, as well as travelling and keeping track of this place.

On behalf of current and former senators, I thank you, David, for your many years of dedicated service to the Senate of Canada, and we all wish you the best for a most enjoyable retirement.

—Tuesday, April 12, 2016

CHNS Radio Halifax

Congratulations on Ninetieth Anniversary

Honourable senators, I rise today to pay tribute to CHNS Radio, in Halifax, Nova Scotia, now known as 89.9 The Wave, which marked its ninetieth anniversary last Thursday.

CHNS Radio made its first broadcast from a tiny room at the Carleton Hotel in Halifax on May 12, 1927, using a 500-watt transmitter. In 1928 the station was acquired by William H. Dennis, who later became a senator, through his Maritime Broadcasting Company. In 1979 Maritime Broadcasting was sold to Maclean Hunter Limited, which increased its holding to six stations and sold in 1994 to a group of Halifax investors headed by Robert L. Pace. Today Maritime Broadcast System Radio comprises 26 radio stations throughout the Maritime provinces.

For the past 90 years this radio station has informed and entertained Haligonians with popular programs such as "Tales Told Under the Old Town Clock," about Nova Scotia history, hosted by Major William C. Borrett, one of the station's founders. Another program, "Atlantic Nocturne," featured reading accompanied by organ music provided by J. Frank Willis. "Uncle Mel" was hosted by Hugh Mills, who would read, using many voices, the comics found in that day's edition of *The Chronicle Herald*. Then there were educational programs such as "ABC Quiz" and "IQ Challenge."

From 1933 to 1960 the station was an affiliate of CBC, and during the Second World War, the Korean War and other major world events, CHNS served as an important broadcast outlet in the Halifax area.

In 2006, CHNS was rebranded, moving from its original 910 on the AM frequency to classic rock music as 89.9 HAL FM, followed by a switch to classic hits and rebirth in 2013 as 89.9 The Wave.

Mike Mitchell, Director of Programming, was quoted as follows in *The Chronicle Herald* last Thursday:

At the heart of it, radio is about putting great storytellers on the air. . . .

Throughout our history, this radio station has told the story of Halifax . . . We've accompanied great music with stories about the city's people, businesses, organizations, and charities. This month, we're celebrating that.

During the entire month of May, listeners will be taken down memory lane with vintage music, historic news stories, commercials, archived interviews and talk shows. If you tune in you can also expect to hear replays of broadcasts by such radio greats as Don Tremaine, Frank Cameron, Stan Carew, Merv Russell and Ian Hanomansing.

We extend our sincere congratulations to CHNS, or as it is now called, 89.9 The Wave; its parent company, Maritime Broadcasting System Radio; and its keen staff as they celebrate 90 years of providing listeners with solid information and entertainment. We wish the station another successful 90 years as it expands and evolves with Facebook, YouTube, Twitter and whatever new means of communication might come along.

—Wednesday, May 18, 2016

The Late Muhammad Ali

Honourable senators, I rise today to pay tribute to the late Muhammad Ali, who departed this life last Friday evening, June 3, at Phoenix, Arizona. He died of septic shock resulting from respiratory problems caused by decades of battling Parkinson's disease, which was as a result of the punishing blows he took to his body and head over his career as perhaps the greatest heavyweight boxer of all time.

Cassius Marcellus Clay, Jr., was born on January 17, 1942, in Louisville, Kentucky. Descended from slaves, he was named after his father, who in turn was named after a staunch Kentucky abolitionist politician. He began boxing at age 12. His six-year amateur career led him to the light heavyweight gold medal in the 1960 Olympic Games in Rome.

He turned professional and began working his way up the rankings. On February 25, 1964, he defeated Sonny Liston to win the world heavyweight title. He proclaimed to all that he was "The Greatest," that he could "float like a butterfly and sting like a bee."

Within months, he shocked the boxing world by announcing that he was embracing Black Muslim leader Malcolm X, that he was a member of the Black Muslims — the Nation of Islam — that he was rejecting his "slave name" and that he would be known as Muhammad Ali.

This was at the height of the civil rights movement in the United States, a time of great racial strife in America. Black Americans had had enough.

Ali tried to claim exemption from the U.S.A.'s military draft, saying that, as a Muslim, he was a conscientious objector, proclaiming, "I ain't got no quarrel with them Vietcong." Many Americans became embittered towards Ali, and on April 28, 1967, he was convicted of draft evasion, stripped of his title and banned from boxing. Although in 1971 the U.S. Supreme Court overturned his conviction on an 8-0 vote, he had sacrificed his best professional boxing years for his beliefs.

Muhammad Ali went on to fight all challengers. He lost a title for the first time in 1971 to Joe Frazier. In two follow-up bouts he defeated Mr. Frazier. In all, Ali won the heavyweight title three times — the only boxer ever to do so.

Among the fights that Ali was taken to the distance in rounds were his two with Canada's George Chuvalo, whom Ali said was "the toughest guy I ever fought."

With the boxing hits taking their toll, Ali retired in 1981, with 56 wins — 37 by knockout — and 5 losses. He then set about becoming the greatest missionary for Islam, travelling the world and meeting heads of state. Indeed, he travelled to Iraq in 1990 and returned with 15 American hostages after speaking to Saddam Hussein. He also gave his time to assist social causes and to help Martin Luther King, Jr., in his work to advance the plight of Black Americans.

Muhammad Ali was "The Greatest" in so many ways, whether in boxing or in pivotal social or political activities. He was one of the most recognized people in the world. We may not see his like again.

—Tuesday, June 7, 2016

World Oceans Day

Honourable senators, on this World Oceans Day, I rise to speak about the Sargasso Sea, which gets its name from the distinctive mats of floating *Sargassum* algae; it's the so-called "golden rainforest of the ocean."

The Sargasso Sea is the world's only non-landlocked body of water, located within the North Atlantic subtropical gyre, bounded on the west by the Gulf Stream, on the north by the North Atlantic Drift, on the east by the Canary Current and on the south by the North Equatorial Current. It's an area of more than 4 million square kilometres.

It's a sanctuary of biodiversity which supports a range of endemic species and plays a critical role in supporting the life cycle of a number of threatened and endangered species, such as the porbeagle shark, billfish, several species of turtle, migratory birds and cetaceans. The *Sargassum* algae mats provide a protective "nursery" for juvenile fish and loggerhead sea turtles. Wahoo, tuna and other pelagic fish also forage in and migrate through this sea, as do a number of whale species, notably the sperm whale and the humpback.

It's also the spawning area for all American and European eels, which then spend their lives in fresh water and migrate thousands of miles back to the Sargasso Sea to spawn. I would advise that these eels, including their elver stage, are a valuable regulated fishery in the Maritime provinces, providing jobs and enhancing our economies.

The Sargasso Sea is under increasing pressure by countless human uses that threaten the habitat and the species it supports. It is faced with several stressors that threaten the long-term viability and health of its ecosystem, such as oil, bilge and ballast water discharge from ships, and concentrations of non-biodegradable plastic waste from ships and land-based sources.

Honourable senators may have heard of the Sargasso Sea Commission, which is a partnership led by the Government of Bermuda in collaboration with other countries, scientists, international marine conservation agencies, marine institutions and private donors. Its members share a mission to protect and manage this unique and vulnerable ocean ecosystem, and to have it established as a Marine Protected Area by way of a declaration signed by supporting countries and international organizations. This Hamilton Declaration was initially signed in Hamilton, Bermuda, on March 11, 2014, by a number of countries, including Bermuda, the United Kingdom and the United States. The commission has a full-time secretariat in Hamilton, Bermuda, and an adjunct office in Washington, D.C.

In closing, honourable senators, it is my hope that Canada will join in this effort to protect the Sargasso Sea and that Canada will be a signatory to the Hamilton Declaration. I humbly ask all honourable senators to canvass friends and colleagues to ensure that Canada, a tri-ocean-bound country, supports the Sargasso Sea protection initiative and becomes a signatory to the Hamilton Declaration.

I invite all honourable senators to visit the website of the commission at www.sargassoalliance.org to learn the importance of protecting this precious and unique open-ocean ecosystem.

—*Wednesday, June 8, 2016*

The Honourable Madam Rosalie Silberman Abella

Congratulations on Honourary Doctorate of Laws Degree

Honourable senators, I rise today to pay tribute to Justice Rosalie Silberman Abella, of the Supreme Court of Canada, upon being awarded an Honourary Doctorate of Laws Degree by Yale University Law School at its convocation held in New Haven, Connecticut, on Monday, May 23, 2016.

Justice Abella, the proud daughter of Jacob and Fanny Silberman, was born in a displaced persons camp in Stuttgart, Germany, on July 1, 1946. Four years later, the family immigrated to Canada, arriving at Pier 21 in Halifax, Nova Scotia.

Her father graduated from Jagiellonian University in Poland in 1934. He articled at a law firm for four years and clerked at a Court of Appeal in Radlow. In July 1939, the Chief Justice of the Court of Appeal approved his candidacy for a judgeship, and the judicial examination was scheduled for October 1939. He had married Fanny on September 3. On the day he was to take the judge's exam, World War II started. He never got to take that exam. He never got to practice law in Poland. Instead, he and his wife spent three years in concentration camps. Their two-year-old son and Jacob's parents and three brothers were all killed at Treblinka.

Upon arriving in Canada, Mr. Silberman applied to the law society to become a member of the bar but was denied because he wasn't a Canadian citizen. In her address to the graduates, Justice Abella said:

> But the moment I heard the story about his being denied the ability to be a lawyer, was the moment I decided to become one. I was four.

Her father died a month before she graduated from law school. He never saw her get called to the bar, never met his two grandsons, and never lived to see her revel in the life of the law. Nevertheless, on Monday in New Haven, she said she felt her father's spirit and his legacy all around her, where she was joined by her all-lawyer support team — husband Irving, sons Jacob and Zachary.

So inspired, she followed her dream and graduated from the University of Toronto with an LL.B. in 1970. She was called to the Ontario Bar in 1972 and practised civil and criminal litigation. In 1976 she was appointed to the Ontario Family Court at the age of 29 — the youngest and first pregnant person appointed to the judiciary in Canada. She was appointed to the Ontario Court of Appeal in 1992. In 2004 she was appointed to the Supreme Court of Canada by Prime Minister Paul Martin. She is the first Jewish female appointed to the Supreme Court.

In delivering the citation, Peter Salovey, President of Yale, applauded Justice Abella for defending the vulnerable in society. He said:

> You defend human rights and justice in your
> home nation of Canada and around the world.
> As one of the world's finest living judges, you
> approach your work with zest, empathy, and
> superb intelligence.

In its 315-year history, Yale has awarded honourary degrees to only four Canadians — all men. Justice Abella became the first Canadian woman to receive this honour.

On behalf of the Senate of Canada we extend our sincere congratulations to Justice Rosalie Silberman Abella. You make us proud!

—Tuesday, June 14, 2016

The Late Robert F. Kennedy

Honourable senators, I rise today to speak about the late Senator Robert Francis Kennedy, affectionately known as "Bobby" and "RFK," the third son of the late Joseph P. Kennedy, Sr., and Rose Elizabeth Fitzgerald Kennedy. June 5 marked the forty-eighth anniversary of his assassination; he died early the next morning from a gunshot to his head. He was 42 years of age and just finished the eighty-second day of his campaign to be his Democratic Party's nominee in the 1968 election for the presidency of the United States.

In 1968 our Senate adjourned on March 27 and no tribute was ever made to Senator Kennedy.

He was a brother of the late President John F. Kennedy, who was assassinated on November 22, 1963. He served as Attorney General in the Kennedy administration and was his brother's principal confidant. He had been elected a senator from the State of New York in 1964.

Bobby announced his presidential candidacy on March 16, 1968, saying that he was running to "close the gaps that now exist between black and white, between rich and poor, between young and old."

His campaign led him to small town main streets, to Black ghettos, to First Nations reserves, to universities, meeting and touching the people on the streets rather than seen only from a TV studio.

He was in Muncie, Indiana, on April 4, 1968 when he learned of the assassination of Martin Luther King, Jr. earlier that day. While reactionary riots were happening in major cities, he chose to speak at a rally in Indianapolis in the worst part of the Black ghetto.

He told the crowd of the death of Dr. King. Emotionally drained, he quieted the crowd as he spoke, saying:

> Let us dedicate ourselves to what the Greeks
> wrote so many years ago: to tame the savageness
> of man and make gentle the life of this world.

Let us dedicate ourselves to that, and say a prayer
for our country and for our people.

Shortly after 7 p.m. on June 5, he arrived at the Ambassador
Hotel in Los Angeles, and with news correspondents awaited the
South Dakota and California primary returns. With the spectacular double victory in hand, he went to the Embassy Ballroom
to thank his supporters. He then headed to the Colonial Room
to meet with print journalists. He went through the hotel pantry
rather than through the frenzied crowd, and while reaching
across a pantry table to shake hands with a kitchen staffer, the
assassin fired his fatal shots.

Bobby's was a campaign of hope. The hope he offered was that
the American people believed in their integrity and that decency
could be restored. His assassination marked not just the death of
another Kennedy and a promising young leader, but the death of
that hope.

His moral imagination was the silent heartbeat of his campaign. It explained why Black Americans considered him their
"blue-eyed soul brother." He became a vigorous advocate for the
rights of Native Americans such that he was adopted into tribes
and given the name "Brave Heart."

With the active support of his wife, Ethel, he campaigned
against the Vietnam War, against poverty, against hunger, against
discrimination. He campaigned for equality, for sharing, offering
hope — always hope.

We can only imagine what good work the Robert F. Kennedy
presidency would have brought to his country and to our world.
I'd like to think there would be no more Sandy Hook, no more
Orlando.

Thank you.

—Thursday, June 16, 2016

Delmore "Buddy" Daye
Learning Institute

Honourable senators, I rise today to pay tribute to the Delmore "Buddy" Daye Learning Institute in Halifax, Nova Scotia. The institute, established two years ago, is a not-for-profit organization committed to improving the educational experiences and outcomes of African-Nova Scotian and African-Canadian students and educators.

The institute is named after Delmore "Buddy" Daye, late of Halifax. He was the Canadian Lightweight Boxing Champion from 1964 to 1966; in his 88 bouts his record was 81 wins — 71 by knockout — 6 losses and 1 draw. He was a founding member of the Black United Front, which sought racial equality in Nova Scotia. He was Canada's first Black Sergeant-at-Arms, serving in the House of Assembly of the Province of Nova Scotia from 1990 until his death in 1995.

Once, when boxing in the United States, a promoter told him to throw the fight and let his opponent win. He would not do that. Upon defeating his opponent, he hurriedly left the U.S. under threat of bodily harm. Such was the integrity of Buddy Daye, and it is that integrity of mission that is the cornerstone of the learning institute that bears his name.

The learning institute is dedicated to excellence in Africentric educational research and practice, with the aim being to advance the academic achievement of African-Canadian students and educators. Its six key program areas are research, policy analysis, curriculum development, professional development, community education, resource and publishing.

The learning institute published its first book, entitled *The Times of African Nova Scotians*, in 2014. This book is now used extensively by educators and is part of the Grade 11 course in African-Canadian Studies across Nova Scotia. It was also one of the three finalists in the Atlantic Book Awards in April 2016, and we congratulate its editor, Tony Colaiacovo.

In closing, honourable senators, I ask that you join with my colleague, Senator Michael MacDonald, and me in commending the Delmore "Buddy" Daye Learning Institute and in encouraging it to continue its good work in improving the education and qualifications of African-Nova Scotian educators and students.

Thank you.

—Wednesday, June 22, 2016

The Late Daniel W. O'Brien, C.M., O.N.B.

Honourable senators, I would also like to join my colleagues in welcoming the new senators, the 14 who were sworn in yesterday and today. Particularly, I'd like to welcome Senator Wanda Bernard, my fellow Nova Scotian. Welcome aboard.

Honourable senators, I rise today to pay tribute to Dr. Daniel W. O'Brien, who departed this life in Halifax, Nova Scotia, on Sunday October 30, 2016. Dan earned a Bachelor of Commerce degree from St. Mary's University, a master's degree from the Maritime School of Social Work and a doctorate in social planning from the University of Pennsylvania.

He was a professor of social work and served as an administrator at Dalhousie University for 21 years. In 1990, Dan was appointed President of St. Thomas University in Fredericton, New Brunswick, and he led that university until 2006. In recognition of his stellar service, in 2010 Dan was installed as St. Thomas University's first President Emeritus, and its principal study hall was named in his honour.

During his time in Fredericton, Dan served on many community boards and committees, including Chair of the Board of the Beaverbrook Art Gallery, during a legacy-defining period. Those good works saw him awarded an honorary Doctorate of Literature from the University of New Brunswick, an induction into the Orders of New Brunswick and Canada, and a papal knighthood.

Following his tenure at St. Thomas University, Dan and his family moved back to Nova Scotia, settling in Chester Basin, where he established an active consulting practice. In 2010, he was appointed Chair of the Halifax Capital District Health Authority Board. He next began a round of important education leadership tasks, including Acting President of the Atlantic School of Theology in 2011 and from 2014-15. He was President of the Nova Scotia College of Art and Design University in Halifax from 2012-14, guiding it through a challenging financial period and developing its "Framework for Stability" document. Upon Dan's passing, Grant Machum, Immediate Past Chair of NSCAD's Board of Governors, said of him:

He is the reason that NSCAD remains
an independent fine arts university with a
worldwide reputation.

Dr. Daniel W. O'Brien leaves behind a legacy of outstanding post-secondary education leadership. He was a true champion, and we are all beneficiaries of his dedicated personable commitment. We extend our heartfelt sympathy to his wife, Valerie, and their sons, Professor Peter and Father Craig.

—*Wednesday, November 16, 2016*

The Late William J. Roué

Honourable senators, I rise to pay tribute to William J. Roué, Canada's premier naval architect, late of Dartmouth, Nova Scotia.

On Thursday, October 26, 2016, I had the pleasure of attending the ceremony at the Canadian Museum of History for the announcement of its acquisition of the William J. Roué collection of artifacts, documents and designs and the establishment of an exhibit of the same. It was a proud day for his descendants.

William J. Roué was born in Halifax in 1879. At four years of age he was already building toy boats, and by 13 was an able skipper. At 16 years of age he had designed a motor boat, Plan Number 1.

In 1907, he was approached by the Vice-Commodore of the Royal Nova Scotia Yacht Squadron in Halifax to design for him a larger boat. Thus Roué designed his first yacht, the Babette, which was launched in 1909 and was still sailing in 1970 out of Long Island, New York. Today she is on display at the Maritime Museum of the Atlantic in Halifax.

After this success his career was under way, and over the next decade he would create 14 more yacht designs, doing so by blueprint, which was then a pioneering concept in North American naval architecture.

In 1920 Bill Roué was chosen to design a vessel for the Bluenose Schooner Company to compete for the International Fishermen's Trophy, which was awarded to the fastest fishing vessel in the North Atlantic. His first design was turned down, as it was longer than requested. With three weeks to go before the deadline to start building, his new design was accepted. It was Roué's Plan Number 17, which bore the name *Bluenose*.

This most famous and successful of all schooner designs not only went on to win the International Fishermen's Trophy five times but did so as a working schooner. She held the record for the largest catch of fish landed in Lunenburg, a true high liner.

We should keep in mind the fact that the *Bluenose* did not race for Lunenburg, nor did she race for Nova Scotia; she raced for Canada. That's why she was the subject of a Canadian stamp in

1929, commonly referred to as the most beautiful stamp by collectors, and that's why she has been on the reverse side of our 10-cent coin since 1937.

For Bill Roué, his career in naval architecture would span many years and over 200 designs, including a type of barge which was used to ferry troops and supplies into Normandy on D-Day.

According to his great granddaughter, Joan Roué, "It has been stated that naval architects must be 75 per cent artist and 25 per cent engineer, and every design, no matter how large or small, must be an inspiration and a labour of love. I wonder if they were describing my great-grandfather and his work when these comments were made."

So, for all of this, William J. Roué and his legacy deserve the national recognition and the status which will come with the establishment of the exhibit in his name, which is scheduled to open at the Canadian Museum of History on July 1, 2017.

—Thursday, November 17, 2016

Viola Desmond

Honourable senators, I rise today to pay tribute to Viola Desmond, late of Halifax, Nova Scotia. Miss Desmond, a Nova Scotian of African descent, was a beauty school entrepreneur; her business was located on Gottingen Street in Halifax.

Upon making a trip to Cape Breton, Miss Desmond stopped in New Glasgow to have her car repaired. While awaiting the repair work to be done, she went to the Roseland Theatre to watch the movie, *The Dark Mirror*, starring Olivia de Havilland.

That theatre had a policy of segregation which required Black patrons to sit in the balcony. Miss Desmond sat in the Whites-only section. Her action caused much turmoil and resulted in her spending the night in jail. Since segregation was then not a law, the next morning Miss Desmond was found guilty of a minuscule violation: failing to pay the one cent tax on the first-floor ticket. She paid the $20 fine and the $6 court costs and drove back to Halifax. Miss Desmond unsuccessfully appealed that conviction.

In 2010, the Province of Nova Scotia apologized for that conviction, posthumously pardoned Miss Desmond and acknowledged that she had the right to resist discrimination.

Miss Desmond's anti-segregation action and her arrest happened on November 8, 1946, nearly a decade before Miss Rosa Parks' historic refusal to give up her seat to a White passenger on a bus in Montgomery, Alabama, on December 1, 1955.

Colleagues, Miss Viola Desmond was a genuine leader of Canada's civil rights movement. Her likeness appeared on a stamp of Canada in 2012, and a Halifax Harbour ferry was named for her earlier this year. She is now on the short list for her image to appear on the next series of banknotes of Canada. It is my hope that this truly Canadian heroine receives that deserved, lasting recognition.

—*Monday, November 28, 2016*

The Late John "Jack" Robert Craig, C.M.

Honourable senators, I rise today to pay tribute to the late John "Jack" Robert Craig, businessman and philanthropist who passed away on October 11, 2016, in Halifax, Nova Scotia, at 86 years of age. Jack was born on the family farm in Cornwall, Ontario. However, he enrolled in the Haileybury School of Mines, leaving the farm for a career in the mining business.

At this time in Kirkland Lake, Jack met a girl named Joan Lewis. They fell in love, eloped and were married in North Bay in 1954. Jack sold mining equipment for the next five years, living in South Porcupine where their son, Robert, was born. While they did not know it, Robert had Asperger syndrome, which would prove difficult at a time when little was known of the condition and there was little or no support.

Joan refused to let Asperger's define Robert's life, and she and Jack worked to support him. Robert has graduated from university and has led his own life, contrary to the opinion of doctors consulted by his parents.

The Craig family settled in Halifax in 1963 where Jack became a salesman for Nova Scotia Tractors and Equipment Limited, steadily working his way up to become its general manager and president. In 1971 Jack took out a loan and bought the company with a colleague, and in 1992 he merged it with one in New Brunswick to form Atlantic Tractors and Equipment. In 1994, Jack was inducted into the Canadian Institute of Mining, Metallurgy and Petroleum; in 1995, the Order of Canada; and in 2000, the Nova Scotia Business Hall of Fame.

His community involvement is renowned. He used his business acumen to rescue many struggling charities. He was a director of the Neptune Theatre and served as president from 1976 to 1978. He was an avid art collector, and his family's financial support for the arts was instrumental in creating a permanent home for the Art Gallery of Nova Scotia, whose board of directors he chaired from 1980 to 1982.

Perhaps the Craig family's greatest contribution was through their leadership on the issue of autism. Their generosity through the Craig Foundation has resulted in the creation of an autism research chair at Dalhousie University. They supported the Autism Research Centre at the IWK Hospital and were instrumental in the founding of Autism Nova Scotia, in 1992. *The Chronicle Herald* newspaper in Halifax put it this way in their 2014 editorial, and I quote:

> As a result of these gifts, Dr. Susan Bryson and
> Dr. Isabel Smith have used the autism chair to
> advance knowledge of diagnosis, treatment and
> early intervention. Autism Nova Scotia has been
> able to provide an array of supports — summer
> camps, job and life skills programs, social groups,
> digital learning devices — that didn't exist
> before. An innovative autism arts program allows
> ASD children, who often experience the world
> through heightened visual and hearing senses, to
> find means of self-expression.

I would like to extend condolences to the Craig family at this time of great loss. I would also like to offer sincere thanks. Nova Scotia is a better place because of Jack Craig. He shall be missed.

—*Thursday, December 1, 2016*

The Hamilton Declaration

Honourable senators, I rise today to inform this chamber that Canada has signed the Hamilton Declaration, becoming the eighth country to commit to preserving the unique ecosystem that is the Sargasso Sea. The Sargasso Sea is the ecological crossroads of the Atlantic Ocean. It is home to several ecological systems and provides the breeding and feeding ground for many species, such as eels, turtles, whales and marlin. Known as a "floating golden rainforest," the *sargassum* seaweed native to this area supports over 150 invertebrate species, as well as 10 species which are found only in the Sargasso Sea. The well-being of the Sargasso Sea is very important for Canada, as it is the birthplace of all *American* eels which find their way to Canada and provide stock for our regulated eel fishery.

However, due to its location in the open ocean, the Sargasso Sea is beyond the jurisdiction of any national government, and thus there exists little in the way of protection for this delicate ecosystem. Bermuda decided to promote the protection of the Sargasso Sea within its own Economic Exclusion Zone as well as on the High Seas.

The creation of the Sargasso Sea Alliance and the resulting permanent commission in Hamilton were the result of Bermuda's collaboration with other conservation-minded countries, marine science organizations and concerned individuals.

It has been my good fortune to have been a participant in the advancement of the Sargasso Sea Alliance. I first spoke about the Sargasso Sea in this chamber on June 4, 2013. That November, I had the opportunity to assist in the drafting of the Hamilton Declaration at a meeting of nations in Tarrytown, New York. I did so under the direction of our former Speaker and colleague, the Honourable Noël Kinsella.

And just this past weekend, I joined our Minister of Fisheries, Oceans and the Canadian Coast Guard, the Honourable Dominic LeBlanc, at the United Nations Biodiversity Conference in Cancun, Mexico, to witness Canada signing the Hamilton Declaration. Mr. Pierre Alarie, Ambassador of Canada to Mexico; and the Honourable Cole Simons, Minister of the Environment of

Bermuda, were also in attendance. It was a great day for Canada on the international stage, but more importantly it's another sign that the conservation and protection of our planet for future generations is firmly on the radar of Canada's government.

I dedicate this statement to Dr. Richard Rockefeller, late of Falmouth, Maine, and David Shaw, of Portland, Maine, the persons who brought the unique ecosystem of the Sargasso Sea to the attention of the world.

—Tuesday, December 6, 2016

Government of The Right Honourable Lester B. Pearson

Fiftieth Anniversary

Honourable senators, I rise today to mark the fiftieth anniversary of the remarkable accomplishments of the Liberal minority government of the late the Right Honourable Lester B. Pearson. Between 1965 and 1966, the Pearson government laid down the foundations of a Canadian society which cares for its own.

The Canada Labour Code was passed in 1965, creating working standards within federal jurisdiction. It created a 40-hour workweek. It put into law overtime pay. It created paid statutory holidays. It created vacation pay. It put into law a minimum wage.

The Canada Assistance Plan, negotiated deftly and cooperatively with the provinces, developed a cost-sharing agreement between the two levels of government which, as the legislation states, would "further the development and extension of assistance and welfare services programs throughout Canada by sharing more fully with the provinces in the cost," which was based on a concern for "the provision of adequate assistance to and in respect of persons in need," and for "the prevention and removal of the causes of poverty and dependence on public assistance."

The Old Age Security Act was amended in order to provide for a Guaranteed Income Supplement, which was directed at those who needed it the most. This enabled some 600,000 pensioners to receive an extra $30 a month and a guaranteed income of $1,260 per year.

The Health Resources Fund laid down the physical foundation providing for the delivery of the Medical Care Act. The fund provided assistance to the provinces to build the infrastructure needed to make medicare function properly. This resulted in the construction and renovation of hospitals, training facilities and research institutions.

The Medical Care Act, which was passed in the House of Commons 50 years ago this past Thursday, December 8, laid out the four guiding principles of universal coverage, public administration, portability and comprehensiveness which formed the basis of Canada's public health system. This of course is the program that Canadians remain most proud of for it has changed for the better so many lives.

Senators, many people played important roles in these great achievements. I'd like to point out one particular individual who was the minister responsible for all of the portfolios involved, the Honourable Allan J. MacEachen. He turned 95 years of age this past July 6, and I can report that he is well and is ensconced in Lake Ainslie, Nova Scotia. I would like to recognize him for a lifetime of dedicated service and devotion to the public good.

—Monday, December 12, 2016

Tributes

The Honourable Wilfred P. Moore

The Hon. the Speaker: Honourable senators, I have received a notice from the Leader of the Opposition who requests, pursuant to rule 4-1, that the time provided for the consideration of Senators' Statements be extended today for the purpose of paying tribute to the Honourable Senator Wilfred Moore, who will be retiring from the Senate on January 14, 2017.

I remind senators that pursuant to our Rules each senator will be allowed three minutes and may speak only once. The list of senators to give tribute is currently quite long, and if everyone takes their full three minutes it would be greatly appreciated.

Honourable senators, is it agreed that we will continue our tributes to Senator Moore under Senators' Statements?

Hon. Senators: Agreed.

Hon. Peter Harder (Government Representative in the Senate): Colleagues, when I first arrived in this chamber nine months ago, one of the first senators I met was Senator Moore. I must say, in the spirit of *Mr. Smith Goes to Washington*, I thought he looked the part. It took only a few encounters for me to realize that he played the part as well.

When you look at his compassion, his sense of justice and his love of Nova Scotia, his causes have become associated with him in a way that all senators would wish their careers to be identified. His commitment to remedying historical injustices with regards to the Aboriginal community; his drive to protect people in their engagement, shall I say, with border and customs officials; and his work on all aspects of justice, policy and individual advocacy are admirable. Last week, he was able to speak in the chamber about the Hamilton Declaration on Collaboration for the Conservation of the Sargasso Sea in the Atlantic Ocean, a subject matter that has preoccupied him for a number of years and that would not have been signed by Canada but for his efforts. We should acknowledge that, even as we say farewell.

I would also note that as the Lorax speaks for trees, Senator Moore speaks for whales. That takes heart. I won't prejudice the outcome of the committee's engagement on Bill S-203, but I think we can all agree that in Senator "Free Willy" Moore, whales have a friend.

As he retires from the Senate, we know that his contributions will be ongoing. In this respect, his efforts that are still under way in the Senate will be memorialized by our respect for how we deal with these bills. Thank you.

Hon. Joseph A. Day (Leader of the Senate Liberals): Honourable senators, I rise to pay tribute to our colleague Senator Wilfred Percy Moore on the occasion of his retirement from the Senate, having not that long ago celebrated his twentieth anniversary as the honourable senator from Stanhope St. / South Shore, Nova Scotia.

We are frequently treated to statements from Senator Moore about the outstanding work of his fellow Nova Scotians, and I am pleased that we will have an opportunity today to recognize his own outstanding contributions.

It is our role as senators to examine legislation and provide sober second thought, but Senator Moore is a notable example of the impact that a senator can have in the creation of legislation, as well. In fact, as we saw yesterday with his introduction of a new bill, he's not prepared to let a little matter like retirement get in the way of advancing issues of importance — in this case, promoting the arts.

One of Senator Moore's earlier initiatives was his bill to amend the Financial Administration Act with respect to borrowing authority. That bill was introduced five times in this chamber. I encourage our newest colleagues to read some of the excellent speeches he gave on the subject matter and the problems with respect to omnibus bills that were related to that particular bill.

Senator Moore doggedly pursued this issue of accountability and was rewarded for his efforts when Finance Minister Bill Morneau decided to incorporate his bill in the budget bill that we passed in June this year.

Of course, I would be remiss if I didn't mention, as Senator Harder has, the "Free Willy" bill that is now before our Standing Senate Committee on Fisheries and Oceans. Senator Moore is a dedicated champion of the issue of whale and dolphin exploitation and has done tremendous work on this file.

Additionally, Senator Moore told this chamber just last week about Canada signing the Hamilton Declaration and the important role that he had the opportunity to play in ensuring the protection of the Sargasso Sea.

These are but a few examples of some of the tremendous achievements that Senator Moore has accomplished as a member of this place. I trust that more will be detailed as others pay tribute to the legacy he has created.

Senator Moore, you have shown us how great of an impact a senator can have through hard work and dedication. I look forward to seeing what retirement will bring for you, and I'm sure I'm not alone in believing that we haven't seen the end of you, sir.

Thank you very much.

Hon. Claude Carignan (Leader of the Opposition): Colleagues, allow me to stand today in tribute to Senator Wilfred P. Moore, who will be retiring on January 14, 2017, during adjournment of the Senate.

On September 26, Senator Moore celebrated his 20th anniversary in the Senate.

For 20 years, Senator Moore worked on behalf of Nova Scotia, the Atlantic region and Canadians in general. For those of us who have been here long enough to see him in action, we know how tenacious he can be. As a former Leader of the Government, I can attest to the fact that facing him in Question Period was never easy. He was always well prepared, to the point, with tough questions — very tough questions. While in opposition, Senator Moore showed us how important the role of the Senate is in keeping the government accountable.

Unfortunately, I didn't have the opportunity to work as closely with Senator Moore as I would have liked. I say unfortunately because I know that he is a gracious, intelligent, warm and very compassionate man. He is in politics to do good things and to make a difference in people's lives.

He is also a man who pays close attention to what's going on in people's personal lives. Senator Moore often asked me how my family and kids were doing. For example, he was aware that I'd had to file an injunction so that my kids could keep going to the school where I was representing a group of 300 students. He frequently asked me how the reintegration was going. That's a great example of how Senator Moore takes a personal interest in people and pays attention to the little details that make up our lives. That is one of Senator Moore's remarkable personality traits.

Here's another example. Do some research on Senator Moore, and you'll find out about this:

In March 2001, the Senator commenced an Inquiry in the Senate on the role of the federal government in the financing of deferred maintenance costs in Canada's post-secondary education institutions. This inquiry, after being considered by the Senate Standing Committee on National Finance, resulted in the federal government providing assistance of $200 million in its 2002 budget for Canada's post-secondary education institutions for the indirect costs of research, which includes the maintenance of the buildings of those institutions. This financial assistance has since continued in every subsequent federal budget as a line item.

Honourable senators, that's a great example of how we, like Senator Moore, can make a difference in society when we make good use of the tools the Senate makes available to us. Senator Moore, your style and your dedication are an example to us all.

I would like to thank you very sincerely for all that you have done for Canadians. I hope that your retirement will be the perfect opportunity to spend special moments with your family, and that you can fully enjoy the world of art, as that is your passion, Senator Moore. Thank you very much.

Hon. James S. Cowan: Colleagues, I am delighted to have an opportunity to say a few words today about my friend, colleague and fellow Nova Scotian, Senator Wilfred Moore.

Senator Moore and I have known one another since we were in high school together in Halifax, and that wasn't yesterday.

Through all those years Senator Moore has provided strong leadership in a wide variety of fields: in public service at the municipal, provincial and federal levels and, through his work with the Canada-U.S. Inter-Parliamentary Group, internationally as well; in the arts, where he and his wife Jane have been benefactors of and advocates for many artistic and cultural events;

in academia, where he has been a strong supporter of both his *alma mater*, Saint Mary's University, and NSCAD University, both of which have recognized his contributions by awarding him honourary degrees.

But for me, Senator Moore's dedication to his community is best exemplified by his almost single-handed saving of the *Bluenose II*. At a time when this iconic symbol of Nova Scotian craftsmanship and history was destined for the scrap heap, he stepped up to establish the *Bluenose II* Preservation Trust Society, mobilize public support, take over the vessel, restore, manage and operate it for 10 years until the provincial government of the day — unwisely, in my view — assumed ownership and control.

In the Senate, we have witnessed that same dogged determination and single-minded focus in his work here — currently, as we've heard, with his whale protection bill, and recently, with his work on the bill which resulted in the return of parliamentary oversight of borrowing by government.

Senator Moore, as we know, never, ever gives up.

May I close by paying tribute to him as a colleague. Throughout my term as leader of our caucus I could not have asked for a more loyal or hard-working colleague. He always provided wise counsel and sound advice, whether I wanted it or not, and even when it might not have been exactly what I wanted to hear. But I appreciated it nonetheless.

Willie, I wish you a long, healthy and active retirement after you and I leave here next month. Godspeed, my friend.

Hon. Jane Cordy: Honourable senators, I am also pleased to speak today about Senator Wilfred Moore and the exceptional contribution he has made not only to the Senate of Canada but especially to the people of Nova Scotia. However, I cannot say that I am pleased that you are retiring, Willie, because I will miss our political discussions when we solved many of the country's problems, and I will miss our shared cab rides to the airport. But most of all, Willie, I will miss your friendship of over 25 years.

We first worked together during Mr. Chrétien's leadership campaign in 1990. You were the campaign chair for Nova Scotia, and Bob and I were on the Nova Scotia team. The convention was in Calgary at the Saddledome, and while I know it is more democratic to have one member, one vote for electing party leaders, I have to say that those old fashioned leadership conventions were exciting because just about anything could happen, and often did. Of course, maybe it had something to do with the fact that we were much younger then and could survive on only a few hours of sleep every night.

We also worked hard on the federal election teams in 1993 and 1997, and, as I recall, you and Robert Pace spent election day in Shawinigan with Mr. Chrétien in 1993, which I am sure was a memorable time.

Before our independence day, when we were part of the caucus with the Liberal MPs, you served as vice-chair of the Nova Scotia and Atlantic caucuses. Do you remember the morning that the Nova Scotia caucus was having our official picture taken with Mr. Ignatieff? Just as the photo was being taken, you pulled out a Saint Mary's University poster, so our caucus photo became an unofficial infomercial for Saint Mary's, which was great for you and Senator Mercer but not so great for Senator Cowan and me, who graduated from Dalhousie and Mount Saint Vincent.

Of course, Willie has been active in promoting his *alma mater*: He established an endowment at Saint Mary's, creating the Senator Wilfred P. Moore Bursary, which provides a $1,000 bursary to a first-year student in the Sobey School of Business.

In recognition of his work with the university, his community and the province of Nova Scotia, Senator Moore was awarded an honourary Doctorate of Laws degree in 2007 by Saint Mary's.

Senator Moore also received an honourary Doctorate of Fine Arts from the Nova Scotia College of Art and Design in 2014. Senator Moore established the Community Studio Residency program in Lunenburg. The program offers recent graduates of NSCAD the opportunity to develop their talents. Willie, your contributions to the arts in Nova Scotia are invaluable.

Senator Moore was the volunteer chairman of the *Bluenose II* Preservation Trust Society. In 1994, the *Bluenose* was deemed to be not seaworthy and unable to sail. Senator Moore and Gerry Godsoe started fundraising to refurbish the *Bluenose*. Not only did they raise the funds, but the *Bluenose II* was ready to serve as Nova Scotia's sailing ambassador when Nova Scotia hosted the

G7 in 1995. If later governments had listened to the wise counsel of Senator Moore instead of playing politics, a lot of anguish and money could have been saved in the recent rebuilding project.

Senator Moore served as an alderman in Halifax and was a founding director and chairman of the Halifax Metro Centre. He is well known as a supporter not only of the arts but of many community activities, including the establishment of a scholarship in the name of his friend, Graham Downey. He was also very active in the efforts to rebuild St. John's Anglican Church in Lunenburg, which was destroyed by fire in 2001.

Willie was named to the inaugural class of the Maritime Sport Hall of Fame in 2014 as a member of the 1961-62 Halifax Kingfishers Junior A hockey team. He was also a member of the Saint Mary's University hockey team.

Senator Moore, you have an eclectic range of interests: sports, the arts, marine animals in captivity, the environment and, of course, politics.

Willie, I applaud you for your contributions to our province of Nova Scotia and our great country of Canada.

I know that you are retiring from this place, but I know that you have more than enough community projects to keep you busy. Bob and I wish you and your wife Jane and your children Nicholas and Alexandra all the best.

Hon. Pierrette Ringuette: Honourable senators, when Senator Moore was appointed to the Senate in 1996, I was an MP in the other place. We both sat in the Liberal Atlantic caucus and the Liberal national caucus.

How times have changed in 20 years, but, fortunately, Senator Moore has always been true to his principles and to the issues he has so vehemently promoted.

His time and devotion to keep and to maintain one of Nova Scotia's iconic symbols, the *Bluenose II*, is an example to us all.

His time and devotion within the Canada-U.S. Inter-Parliamentary Group kept Atlantic Canada in touch with its neighbour and almost sole trading partner.

Willie has been an example of dedication to Nova Scotia and to Atlantic Canada. He fought for fairness, from post-secondary education to banking, from food banks to small businesses.

In his 20 years on Parliament Hill, Willie has pursued issues persistently and always as a gentleman, as a diplomat.

I must thank you particularly for your unwavering support with regard to merchant credit card fees. Willie would keep me informed on what was developing in the U.S. and would send me U.S. media clippings on a regular basis. Thank you, Willie.

Dear Senator Moore, my friend, if you grew a beard in your retirement, you would be an amazing Santa Claus. Today, you are even wearing the right necktie. That being said, Santa Claus or not, you have been a gift to the Senate and to all Canadians.

I do not believe that Santa Claus can retire, so you have to continue to give, Willie. And I know that you will. I wish you the best of health, and, last but not least, be very, very careful with those chimneys.

I will miss you, my friend. Thank you.

Hon. Terry M. Mercer: Honourable senators, the Honourable Senator Dr. Wilfred P. Moore, Q.C., has been a friend of mine for over 40 years. It's an honour to rise to say a few words about him. Don't worry, Willie, I'm not going to tell some of those embarrassing stories I might have.

Wilfred P. Moore has had quite a life and an amazing career. He is a proud Haligonian. Saint Mary's University conferred a Bachelor of Commerce degree on Willie in 1964 and Dalhousie a law degree in 1968. I like the first degree better, of course, because it's from Saint Mary's University, our *alma mater*, and a place where Willie has done such good work, including serving on the board of governors.

He also was awarded a Doctorate of Law degree by Saint. Mary's and an Honourary Doctorate of Fine Arts degree from the Nova Scotia College of Art and Design University, all in recognition of his work as a tireless supporter for universities and their students.

Willie cut his political teeth as an alderman with the City of Halifax. He also ran provincially for the Liberal Party in Nova Scotia. He had quite a team, women like Betty Murphy,

Betty Fry and my aunt Evelyn Mercer. What a team they were. They ran Fairview like they owned it.

While I was Executive Director of the Liberal Party of Nova Scotia, Willie was Treasurer. Then he became the Vice-President of Policy and eventually the President. During that time, we initiated some very important spending and fundraising reforms that directly influenced the course of the Liberal Party politically in Nova Scotia.

It was a great time to be a Liberal, and I would suggest it still is. A small group of us had a lot of fun during that time and had many adventures. There are many stories that I will not utter here, of course. Suffice to say that Willie was always there to offer his help, his advice and certainly his opinion. We all listened every time he did.

I do believe his most important work outside of politics was that of Chairman of the *Bluenose II* Preservation Trust. I am most sure that there would not be as many problems with the current incarnation of the vessel if Willie were still in charge.

In his spare time, which he doesn't have much of, Willie has also been involved in a successful art business. Indeed, I have two prints hanging on my walls at home that came from Willie's efforts there. He's also done some great work with the brand new Lunenburg School of the Arts as chairman of the board. There is not enough time to talk about the many achievements in the Senate since being appointed by the Right Honourable Jean Chrétien in 1996. It was interesting: Willie told me that, on his twentieth anniversary in the Senate, he picked up the phone and called Mr. Chrétien and said, "Boss, I just called to say thank you." Mr. Chrétien said, "What are you thanking me for?" He said, "I am thanking you for appointing me 20 years ago today to the Senate." That's the kind of guy Willie is.

Senator Moore's work on Canada-U.S. relations is certainly a highlight. Anybody who has been involved in the Canada-U.S. Inter-Parliamentary Group knows that Willie has always been one of the leaders, and his work has been extraordinary.

Honourable senators, I know this is the end of Willie's career in the Senate, but it's not the end of our friendship or the many friendships he has made over the years in this place.

Congratulations on a successful career, my friend. We all look forward to seeing what you do next.

Hon. Serge Joyal: Senator Moore, I would like to speak to your sense of humanity and what the Senate owes you.

I had the opportunity to be in this chamber for many years and share several experiences with you, and there are two fights that you led that I would like to acknowledge today.

The first one happened in 1999, on the extradition bill. You will remember that bill, introduced by the Minister of Justice of the day, a minister of the Liberal Party. The bill contained no provision to save the life of persons who would be extradited to countries where the death penalty would be imposed.

We had to fight the Minister of Justice to amend that bill, and the debate lasted for more than three months in the Senate Chamber, against all the odds of the government trying to lobby the senators, directly or indirectly, to force their vote in support of the bill. You remember that pressure, senator?

I want to remember that fight in those days because we're talking about independence of senators. I think you did show the kind of independence of mind that was at the forefront of your commitment to your personal values and to your principles. I want to acknowledge that.

I also want to mention the fight that you led in 2003 on the Youth Criminal Justice Bill. Do you remember that one, Senator Moore? You introduced an amendment to protect Aboriginal youth who found themselves in court and to get from the courts the same kind of consideration that adult Aboriginal people would get on the sentencing provision of section 7.18 of the bill. The hope was that the *Gladue* protection would make sure that the courts would pay due consideration to the status of an Aboriginal youth.

We won by one vote, and I remember very well how it happened. It was Senator Hervieux-Payette, who happened to run from Montreal to be here just on time before the vote was called. We won that vote. We changed the Youth Criminal Justice Bill to make sure that Aboriginal youth would be paid due consideration in our system of justice, considering the past and the plight that the Aboriginal people had to suffer in Canada.

I want to acknowledge you, Senator Moore, and say to all colleagues in the chamber that our independence of mind is the first quality that any one of us is called upon to show when we are confronted with important issues pertaining to the plight of those who are exploited or have not been given a chance in history, or those who are faced with the plight of the death penalty.

We are also indebted to you, Senator Moore, to have supported the history of our chamber and your commitment to ensure that the institution of the Senate and the constitutional monarchy in which we live have been appreciated by our colleagues.

Look at the calendar on the table. It's due to you. I remember very well in 2012 when we decided to honour the Diamond Jubilee of the Her Majesty the Queen. Former Senator Fortin-Duplessis and you volunteered to pass the hat on both sides of the chamber, and each one of us donated money to be sure that we would be able to honour our Queen, the Queen of Canada, in that jubilee year.

Thank you, Senator Moore. You are a lasting example for our future.

Hon. Mobina S. B. Jaffer: Honourable senators, I rise to pay tribute to our colleague and dear friend Senator Moore, Q.C.

The work Senator Moore has done through the various avenues he has access to, whether through one of his roles with the Liberal Party, where I first met him, or as a lawyer or the tireless worker that he has been in the chamber, clearly show that he has committed his professional life to improving the lives of all Canadians. He has worked tirelessly for us. It is because of the spirit of service that Senator Moore embodies that I respect and admire his work, both as a colleague and on a personal level.

Over the years, we have watched Senator Moore lead by example, showing how to help change a country. You have to participate. Only by showing up can you have an impact on your communities, and show up for his community he did. That is why he's so fondly known in Halifax and now in this chamber.

By focusing on his own community so consistently, Senator Moore embodies the truth we all try to live by: Service starts in our own backyards.

Every institution Senator Moore has been a part of has benefited from his opinions, thoughts and contributions. And every institution has felt that Senator Moore is an active member of the community, involved, bringing a sense of trust to the opinions he expressed — they were personal. Senator Moore, you really care about Canadians, and I want to thank you for that.

Senator Moore's contributions have been as vast and diverse as our country itself, and through all of his work we see that consistent theme of supporting, uplifting and improving a community. It started in Halifax, but he has managed to extend that sentiment across the entire country to the community of Canada.

Senator Moore, we thank you for your leadership by example. We thank you for your passion, and we thank you for your years of tireless service. This chamber will miss you, but we take comfort knowing that your presence will still be felt through the impact of your work over the last years, both here and across our great nation.

Senator Moore, Jane Cordy and I will miss the dinner dates we had with you. We will truly miss this.

Senator Moore, I will miss you. Now, my friend, it is time to have some fun.

Hon. Dennis Dawson: I think I'm the last to speak. Willie, I always told you after having been your seatmate for many years that I would have the last word because you were leaving before me. This is it. No, I will be very short.

Sometimes we have activities outside of the public, and in Willie's case he was co-chair of the legislative committee of the Liberal caucus, the national caucus, in the good old days, like we say. And Willie would be the one who would assure us that we would not have the type of issues that we have had over the last few weeks, including the last week on a bill like Bill C-29, when the national caucus and the house chamber and the Senate Chamber would be able to cooperate to avoid the type of confrontation that we have had over the last few months. That's the unseen side of my friend Willie Moore, who was a party insider and a very active party insider.

Well, we would often disagree, but we did work in the best interests of our party.

I know one thing Willie does love is Charlevoix, Baie-St.-Paul and Le Massif. So I hope now that he is retiring I can have the opportunity, since I will also be feeling better over the next few weeks, to invite you to come to Le Massif and I can maybe finish off by being able to teach you how to snowboard so that you can profit from the hills of Le Massif and the 90 inches of powdered snow we have this year. You can see the whales off Tadoussac. That will be very appropriate for you.

I want to thank you, mon ami, for having been my seat-mate and trying to control me sometimes when I was a little bit mischievous. Merci, mon ami.

—*Tuesday, December 13, 2016*

The Honourable Wilfred P. Moore

Hon. Charlie Watt:
[*Editor's note: Senator Watt spoke in Inuktitut.*]
I rise to say a few words about our former colleague, Willie Moore, who retired before I had a chance to say goodbye.

We've known each other since 1996, when he was appointed to the upper chamber, and I have tremendous respect for his work. In particular, his interest in the North and indigenous communities has been great. As the only Inuk senator in the country, it can be lonely for me. He was a great advocate for indigenous people, and his well-informed and thoughtful contributions to the committee are much appreciated.

Willie puts a lot of attention into everything that he does, and that includes his preparation for the Standing Senate Committee on Aboriginal Peoples. As a newcomer to the committee, he was able to inject fresh and meaningful perspectives on the issues. His concern over our housing issues and the need for improved living conditions was admirable.

We will miss Willie's considerate nature and his contributions on behalf of indigenous people. He is a great example of how we can work together for the betterment of our under-represented communities.

[*Editor's note: Senator Watt spoke in Inuktitut.*]

Thank you, Willie, and best wishes for your new adventures. *Nakurmiik.*

Hon. Elizabeth Hubley (Deputy Leader of the Senate Liberals): Honourable senators, I am very pleased to have the opportunity to pay tribute to my friend and our former colleague, the Honourable Willie Moore. I had been so disappointed to be travelling during the time for his official tributes, so I am glad he has come today to peer down on us.

I know many before me spoke at length about Willie's achievements here in the Senate and in his beloved Nova Scotia. But as a dancer, artist and fiddler, I have a special place in my heart for the arts, and I know very well that Willie does, too. I want to highlight some of those contributions.

We know that Willie was a dedicated volunteer at the Nova Scotia College of Art & Design, and was recognized with an honourary Doctorate of Fine Arts for NSCAD in 2014.

He also initiated the establishment of NSCAD's Community Studio Residency program in Lunenburg, which offers recent graduates donated studio space in the town. Willie said later that he pitched the idea to the then-NSCAD president as: "I want you to open a facility in Lunenburg. You are the Nova Scotia College of Art and Design after all, not the Halifax College of Art and Design." As always, he was right, and now NSCAD offers its residency program in Sydney, New Glasgow and Dartmouth.

A few years ago, he helped form the Lunenburg School of the Arts and now serves as the chair of its board of directors. The school offers workshops to kids and to students of all ages in areas like pottery, drawing, writing and photography. Willie recently told the Halifax *Chronicle Herald* that he looks forward to spending more time volunteering there. He is passionate about working with young people in the arts, and this school offers a wonderful start to those children who participate.

Willie Moore has done more than his fair share to help foster Nova Scotian and Canadian art, and I would say that his work is just beginning.

Thank you, Willie, and best of luck to you, Jane, Alexandra and Nicholas, as you take on this next chapter in your life.

—Wednesday, February 8, 2017

The Honourable Wilfred P. Moore

Expression of Thanks

Wow. Thank you, honourable senators, for your generous remarks. Needless to say, I shall miss you all. I shall really miss this Red Chamber. The opportunities that this place presents are unbelievable. Every day when I enter this place I never take it for granted. It has been an honour to be here and to participate in our precious democratic process.

Upon my appointment — I just had Charles Robert look this up — I was the eight hundred and first Canadian to ever sit in this chamber. I mean, what an honour. This leads me to thank the Right Honourable Jean Chrétien for appointing me to the Senate, and I hope that I have honoured his judgment in making that appointment.

My heartfelt thanks go to my family, my wife Jane, our son Nicholas and our daughter Alexandra, and I am most grateful for their patience during my many absences while attending to my Senate responsibilities, and for their steadfast love and their encouragement for me to do the right thing and to do my job.

I want to thank my hard-working staff, who toiled alongside me in the best interests of Canada, the late Doralen Amesbury, Lisa Fisher, Marie Russell and Archie Campbell. Archie possesses consummate political antennae and is an outstanding writer.

I also thank my A-team: Sheldon Gillis, Vincent McNeil, David Murphy and Archie Campbell for their strategic advice, their encouragement and their friendships. No finer group of Cape Bretoners has ever crossed the causeway. All of you have made me look good, and I'm very grateful for that.

Others whom I wish to thank: the table officers for their service and advice over the years; the various pages over the years; also my thanks to the numerous committee clerks with whom I have worked, and to the reporters and translators; thank you to the security service, their courteous assistance, even letting me in my office when I forgot my key; and a special thanks to our editing and transcribing service, particularly D'Arcy McPherson and Janet Lovelady, with whom I have worked in getting out my

Senator Statements and speeches. They have been very helpful to me over the years.

Another group who has my utmost gratitude and thanks are the staffs in the parliamentary restaurant, the fifth-floor cafeteria and the little cafeteria in the East Block for keeping me fuelled up so I can do my work. I also want to thank my seatmates, past and present, for putting up with me and for sharing many personal anecdotes.

The Senate provides special opportunities to make Canada a better place. I'm relieved and pleased that we are maintaining the process of appointing members to this chamber. It ensures that our regions and our minorities are well and properly represented. However, I sorely miss Wednesdays, those days of the past when we all sat as Liberals in caucus and shared stories and strategized as colleagues. I really miss those days.

I also miss Shelagh Cowan's oatmeal cookies, Jim.

With regard to our many new Senate colleagues, I urge you to seize the opportunities and to immerse yourselves in issues that you hold close. I further urge you to get involved with one or more of the parliamentary groups.

The Canada-United States Inter-Parliamentary Group was of deep interest to me. It presented unique opportunities to engage with our largest trading partner, our neighbour to the south, and our ally. The network of friendships with our counterpart legislators is most important. I want to thank June Dewetering for her professional assistance and guidance during those years. June is with the Library of Parliament, and a real pro.

In closing, this has been a most rewarding experience for me. I have left my fingerprints on some pieces of good legislation, on an international agreement and on some programs that assisted my province and Atlantic Canada, particularly regarding post-secondary education. It was also a joy to serve in the Senate's Artwork Advisory Working Group and to leave behind some lasting enhancements.

Honourable colleagues, my time in the Senate comes to an end at midnight on January 13, 2017. In the words of my friend the late Johnny Cash, "I don't like it, but I guess things happen that way." Au revoir, mes amis. . . till we meet again.

—Tuesday, December 13, 2016